unhitched
The Ultimate Divorce Survival Guide

SANDY MAECK

Author - * Life and Health Coach * - Toronto

Instagram: @sandy_maeck

Facebook: Maeck Shobha

Email: sandy@sandymaeck.com

Website: www.sandymaeck.com

First published by Ultimate World Publishing 2025
Copyright © 2025 Sandy Maeck

ISBN

Paperback: 978-1-923425-47-7
Ebook: 978-1-923425-48-4

Sandy Maeck has asserted her rights under the Copyright, Designs and Patents Act 1988 to be identified as the author of this work. The information in this book is based on the author's experiences and opinions. The publisher specifically disclaims responsibility for any adverse consequences which may result from use of the information contained herein. Permission to use information has been sought by the author. Any breaches will be rectified in further editions of the book.

All rights reserved. No part of this publication may be reproduced, stored in or introduced into a retrieval system, or transmitted in any form, or by any means (electronic, mechanical, photocopying, recording or otherwise) without the prior written permission of the author. Any person who does any unauthorized act in relation to this publication may be liable to criminal prosecution and civil claims for damages. Enquiries should be made through the publisher.

Cover design: Ultimate World Publishing
Layout and typesetting: Ultimate World Publishing
Editor: Marnae Kelley

Ultimate World Publishing
Diamond Creek,
Victoria Australia 3089
www.writeabook.com.au

No one's coming to swoop in and save the day—sorry, the cape has been retired!

It's time to get off the sidelines and start creating the life you actually want.

Get up, take charge, and make it happen!

Testimonials

Unhitched: A Survivor's Guide to Divorce is a practical and empowering guide for anyone facing the challenges of divorce. It offers emotional support, financial guidance, and essential advice on custody, co-parenting, and rebuilding relationships. More than just a roadmap through the process, this guide helps you heal, regain control, and step into the next chapter of your life with confidence and clarity.

Susan Persaud, Esq.
Law Offices of Susan N. Persaud & Associates, PLLC
New York

Unhitched: A Survivor's Guide to Divorce is more than just a book—it's a lifeline for anyone facing the emotional and financial upheaval of divorce. With raw honesty and practical wisdom, it offers compassionate support and actionable advice to help readers navigate heartbreak, manage finances, handle child custody challenges, co-parent effectively, and build healthy new relationships. This isn't just about surviving divorce—it's about rising from it, stronger and more empowered than ever.

I am incredibly proud of my wife, Sandy, for writing this book. Before I met her, I went through a divorce myself—a painful, isolating chapter where I often wished for guidance to make sense of the chaos. That's exactly why she wrote *Unhitched*—to ensure no one has to go through divorce feeling lost, broken, or powerless. This book is a beacon of hope, proving that even in life's darkest moments, a new beginning is possible.

Thomas Maeck
Nuclear Services Manager

Unhitched: A Survivor's Guide to Divorce is a compassionate and practical resource for anyone facing the complexities of divorce. Covering everything from emotional healing and financial stability to custody arrangements and rebuilding connections, this book equips readers with the tools to navigate divorce with confidence. More than just a survival guide, it's a roadmap to reclaiming strength, resilience, and a fresh start.

Jacqueline Dixon
CEO New Era Communications
Founder of Meet the Motivators & Resilient Women

Dedicated to the survivors of divorce and those currently going through a divorce

This book is dedicated to all those who have braved the storm of divorce and emerged stronger, and to those still navigating their way through it. It stands as a tribute to your unshakable resilience, your courage, and the relentless strength of your spirit.

Divorce is a journey that can shake the very foundations of our lives, leaving us feeling lost, broken, and uncertain about the future. Yet, amid the chaos, you have demonstrated incredible strength, determination, and the ability to rebuild your life piece by piece.

To the survivors who have navigated the emotional roller coaster, the legal complexities, and the profound changes that divorce brings, this book is for you. It is a tribute to your unwavering spirit and a reminder that you are not alone.

Through these pages, I hope to offer guidance, support, and inspiration. May this book serve as a companion on your path to healing, growth, and finding the silver linings that arise from even the most challenging experiences.

You have shown that divorce does not define you. You are survivors, warriors, and beacons of hope. Your strength and resilience inspire me, and I am honoured to dedicate this book to you.

With heartfelt gratitude and admiration,

Sandy Maeck

Contents

Testimonials	vii
Dedicated to the survivors of divorce and those currently going through a divorce	ix
Introduction	1
CHAPTER ONE: Coping with the Emotional Fallout	7
CHAPTER TWO: Reinventing Your Identity	51
CHAPTER THREE: Navigating the Single Life	93
CHAPTER FOUR: Navigating Child Custody	103
CHAPTER FIVE: Dating After Divorce	113
CHAPTER SIX: Financial Independence	121
CHAPTER SEVEN: Dealing with Loneliness	139
CHAPTER EIGHT: The Power of Words: Mastering Communication During and After Divorce	151
CHAPTER NINE: Navigating Legal Challenges	157
CHAPTER TEN: Building a Support System	173

CHAPTER ELEVEN: Finding Happiness and Fulfillment — 185
CHAPTER TWELVE: Creating a Positive Co-Parenting Relationship — 195
CHAPTER THIRTEEN: Overcoming Shame and Stigma — 209
CHAPTER FOURTEEN: Redefining Your Relationships — 223
CHAPTER FIFTEEN: Maintaining a Positive Outlook — 233
Embrace the Present with Gratitude — 249
Navigating Divorce with Financial Confidence — 251
Offers — 253
Speaker Bio — 255

Introduction

"Smart women recognize they can't change their ex-husband. They pick their battles, they let go of issues that don't really matter or can't be changed, and they accept with grace and maturity the general unpleasantness of an ongoing custody share—knowing this is just the reality of divorce."

—Alison L. Patton, Esq., HuffPost

I am writing this book about helping women find freedom after divorce because I know that divorce can be an incredibly difficult and painful experience, particularly for women. Many women find themselves feeling lost, alone, and unsure of what to do next. They may feel like they have lost a part of themselves and struggle to find their footing again.

Nevertheless, I hold the perspective that divorce presents an opportunity for personal growth and transformation. It provides a moment to reconnect with one's true self and forge a fresh path aligned with personal values and aspirations. My goal is to assist women in navigating this journey, enabling them to emerge from divorce with a sense of empowerment, confidence, and freedom.

Through my book, I aim to provide practical advice, tools, and resources that women can use to overcome the challenges of divorce and build a fulfilling life on **their terms.** My hope is that this book will offer emotional support and encouragement to women who may be feeling overwhelmed or discouraged during or after divorce.

Recognizing the uniqueness of each individual's journey, I aim to guide women in perceiving divorce as a pathway to a brighter future, rather than a cause of distress. I believe every woman is entitled to lead a joyful and fulfilling life. Through my book, I aspire to offer support and insights to assist women in attaining a more content and satisfying life beyond divorce.

Women who thrive after divorce channel their energy into self-reflection and personal growth. They take the time to assess their lives, set new goals, and learn from past mistakes. Rather than rushing into another relationship or dwelling on their ex, they focus on developing a deeper understanding of themselves. This period of introspection allows them to reevaluate their priorities and rediscover what truly matters to them. They grow into women whose identity is no longer defined by the roles of mother or wife, but by their own passions, ambitions, and unique strengths.

I can relate to this journey of growth. After my own divorce, I realized that I needed to rebuild not just my life, but also my sense of self. It was a difficult process but one that ultimately brought me clarity and strength. I spent time reflecting on past decisions, understanding my needs, and learning from the experiences that shaped me. Instead of rushing into a new relationship, I focused on nurturing my own well-being, exploring new passions, and strengthening my emotional resilience.

Through this process, I rediscovered my worth and began to see myself not just as a wife or mother, but as a powerful, independent woman with her own dreams and goals. I invested in my personal development, which led me to become a certified life and health coach, allowing me to help others navigate their own challenges. This transformation was not easy, but it gave me a renewed sense of purpose, and I now embrace the opportunities for growth that come with every new chapter in life. It was through this self-reflection and empowerment that I learned the importance of putting myself first, of growing beyond my past, and of realizing that I am not defined by any one relationship or role.

What would be on your list for recovery from a divorce?

Recovery from divorce is a deeply personal and unique journey, but there are some common aspects that many individuals find helpful in navigating the healing process. Throughout this book, you will notice me reiterating certain themes and strategies. I believe in their importance, and as we delve deeper into each topic, I feel it's crucial to revisit them. This repetition is intentional, as it emphasizes key principles that can truly aid in your recovery and growth.

- **Prioritize Self-Care:** Focus on your overall well-being by taking care of your physical, emotional, and mental health. Participate in activities that make you happy, whether it's exercising, pursuing hobbies, meditating, attending therapy, or spending quality time with loved ones.

- **Seek Support:** Build a strong support network of friends, family, or support groups who can offer you guidance, encouragement, and a sympathetic ear during this difficult period.

- **Allow Yourself to Grieve:** Allow yourself to experience and process the range of emotions that come with divorce, including sadness, anger, and loss. Give yourself permission to grieve the end of the relationship and the life you once had.

- **Set Boundaries:** Establish healthy boundaries with your ex-partner to create emotional and physical space for your own healing. Clearly communicate your needs and prioritize your well-being as you navigate post-divorce interactions.

- **Focus on Self-Reflection:** Take time to reflect on the lessons learned from your marriage and divorce. Understand your role in the relationship dynamics, identify patterns, and work towards personal growth and development.

- **Let Go of Resentment:** Holding onto resentment and bitterness can hinder your healing process. Practice forgiveness, not for the sake of your ex-partner, but for your own emotional liberation and inner peace.

- **Rediscover Your Identity:** Use this time as an opportunity for self-discovery. Reconnect with your interests, passions, and goals. Explore new hobbies, embark on personal growth activities, or pursue long-held dreams.

- **Achieve Financial Stability:** Secure your financial future by evaluating your current financial status, creating a budget, and seeking professional guidance if needed. Building financial independence can provide a sense of security and empowerment.

- **Parenting Communication:** If you have children, prioritize healthy and open communication with your ex-partner to ensure the well-being of your children.

Focus on cooperation, consistency, and respect in co-parenting decisions.

- **Look to the Future:** Embrace the possibilities that lie ahead. Set new goals, make plans, and envision a fulfilling future for yourself. Recognize that this is a chance for personal growth, reinvention, and the opportunity to create a life that aligns with your values and desires.

Remember, everyone's journey is unique, and there is no timeline for healing. Give yourself the grace and patience needed to heal, and consider seeking professional support from therapists or counselors specializing in divorce recovery if you find it beneficial.

CHAPTER ONE

Coping with the Emotional Fallout

People may experience various emotions after a divorce, such as anger, sadness, and guilt. Coping with the emotional fallout after a divorce can be difficult, but several strategies can help you manage your feelings and move forward.

Allow yourself to feel your emotions. It's important to permit yourself to feel your emotions and not try to suppress them. Allow yourself to grieve the loss of your relationship, feel anger or frustration, and acknowledge your sadness. Remember that it's normal to have a range of emotions after a divorce.

Practice Self-care

Self-care is essential for managing your emotions after a divorce. Take time to engage in activities that make you feel good, such as exercise, meditation, or spending time with friends. Make sure to get enough sleep, eat healthily, and take care of your physical health.

Practicing self-care is essential for maintaining good physical, emotional, and mental health. Here are some tips on how to practice self-care:

- **Get enough sleep:** Aim to get seven to eight hours of sleep each night. Try to establish a regular sleep routine by going to bed and waking up at the same time each day.

- **Eat a healthy diet:** Eat a balanced diet with plenty of fruits, vegetables, whole grains, and lean proteins. Avoid processed and junk foods as much as possible.

- **Exercise regularly:** Engage in regular physical activity that you enjoy, such as yoga, swimming, or jogging. Exercise not only improves physical health but also boosts mood and reduces stress.

- **Practice relaxation techniques:** Find ways to relax and de-stress, such as meditation, deep breathing, or a warm bath.

- **Spend time in nature:** Spending time in nature has been shown to improve mood and reduce stress. Take a walk in the park or go for a hike in the woods.

- **Engage in hobbies and activities you enjoy:** Take time to do things you enjoy, such as reading, painting, or listening to music.

- **Connect with others:** Spend time with friends and family or join a social group or club.

- **Take breaks and schedule downtime:** It's important to take breaks throughout the day and schedule downtime to rest and recharge.

- **Seek professional help when needed:** If you're struggling with mental health issues, don't hesitate to seek professional help from a therapist, coach or counselor.

We will delve deeper into these topics later on.

Remember that self-care is not selfish; it's essential for maintaining good health and well-being. Start by incorporating one or two self-care practices into your routine and gradually build from there. To embark on a journey of self-care, begin by introducing one or two practices into your daily routine. This gradual approach allows you to ease into the process and establish sustainable habits over time. Choose activities that resonate with you and align with your interests, needs, and values. Self-care practices can encompass various aspects of your life, such as physical, emotional, mental, and spiritual well-being.

For physical self-care, consider incorporating activities like regular exercise, nourishing your body with healthy meals, prioritizing sufficient sleep, and engaging in relaxation techniques such as yoga or meditation. Taking breaks throughout the day to stretch or go for a walk can also rejuvenate your body and mind.

Emotional self-care involves nurturing your emotional well-being. You can do this by engaging in activities that bring you joy, spending time in nature, listening to music, journaling, or practicing mindfulness. It's essential to acknowledge and validate your emotions, allowing yourself to feel and process them in a healthy and supportive manner.

Mental self-care focuses on maintaining good mental health. This can involve activities like reading books, learning new skills, engaging in puzzles or brain games, seeking intellectual stimulation, or practicing mindfulness and meditation. Setting boundaries, both in personal and professional relationships, is also crucial for preserving your mental well-being.

Nurturing your spiritual well-being can be an integral part of self-care as well. This can include practices such as meditation, prayer, connecting with nature, engaging in reflection or gratitude exercises, or participating in activities that align with your spiritual or religious beliefs.

Remember, self-care is a journey unique to each individual, and it may evolve and change over time. Be patient and compassionate with yourself as you explore what works best for you. Gradually incorporate additional self-care practices into your routine, allowing them to become ingrained habits that support your overall well-being. By dedicating time and attention to self-care, you are investing in your long-term health and happiness.

Seek Support

Talk to a trusted friend, family member, or therapist about your feelings. Having a support system can help you feel less alone and provide you with a safe space to express yourself. Recognize the significance of seeking support from your loved ones during the healing journey following a divorce. It's essential to remember that you need not face the challenges alone, and reaching out for assistance is an act of strength, not weakness. Embrace the understanding that friends and family can be a vital source of comfort, guidance, and encouragement during this transitional period.

Allow yourself to be vulnerable and open about your emotions. Sharing your feelings with trusted individuals can offer a sense of relief and validation. Those you trust can offer a listening ear, empathetic understanding, and valuable insights that can help you navigate the complexities of post-divorce emotions. Their presence can serve as a reminder that you are not alone in your experiences.

Additionally, engaging in discussions about your emotions with supportive individuals can provide a fresh perspective, enabling you to gain new insights and clarity. Their outside viewpoint can help you process your emotions, and often they can offer guidance in finding healthier ways to cope with the challenges you may be facing.

Remember that seeking support is not a sign of weakness but a courageous step towards self-care and healing. Allow yourself to lean on your support network, trusting that they genuinely want to be there for you. Their presence can bring comfort, reassurance, and a sense of belonging during this transformative phase of your life. Seeking support from friends and family is an important part of the healing process after a divorce. Don't be afraid to reach out for help, and remember that you don't have to go through this alone.

Here are some tips on how to seek help from a friend or relative when going through a divorce:

- **Be honest and open:** Be honest with your friend or relative about what you're going through and how you're feeling. Share your thoughts and feelings openly and don't be afraid to ask for help.

- **Choose the right person:** Choose someone you trust and feel comfortable talking to. It could be a close friend, family member, or even a therapist.

- **Be specific about what you need:** Be clear about what you need from your friend or relative. Do you need someone to listen to you vent, or do you need practical help, for example, with childcare or running errands?

- **Set boundaries:** Let your friend or relative know what you're comfortable with and what your boundaries are. For example, if you don't want to talk about certain topics, let them know.

- **Be mindful of their feelings:** Remember that your friend or relative may also be going through a difficult time. Be mindful of their feelings and try to be considerate of their needs as well.

- **Don't rely solely on one person:** While it's great to have support from a friend or relative, it's important not to rely solely on one person. Consider joining a support group or seeking professional help if you need additional support.

- **Express your gratitude:** Remember to express your gratitude to your friend or relative for their support. Let them know how much you appreciate their help and how much it's meant to you through this difficult time.

Seek Professional Help

Seeking the assistance of a therapist, coach, or counselor can be invaluable when it comes to dealing with the emotional complexities and the challenges that come with divorce. These trained professionals possess the expertise and knowledge to provide you tools, guidance, and support to effectively work through your emotions and facilitate your healing process.

Therapists, coaches, and counsellors create a safe and non-judgmental space where you can freely express your thoughts, feelings, and concerns. They offer a compassionate and empathetic presence, allowing you to explore the emotional impact of your divorce in a supportive environment. Through active listening and effective communication, they help you gain a deeper understanding of your emotions and the underlying factors contributing to your current state.

With their expertise, therapists and counselors can help you develop healthy coping mechanisms and adaptive strategies for managing the challenges that arise during this significant life transition. They provide a toolbox of therapeutic techniques tailored to your specific needs, such as cognitive behavioral therapy (CBT), mindfulness-based interventions, emotion-focused therapy, or narrative therapy. These approaches can help you process your emotions, reframe negative thought patterns, and develop resilience in the face of adversity.

Furthermore, therapists and counselors offer valuable insights and perspectives. They can help you gain clarity and provide objective guidance when making decisions or navigating complex emotions. Their professional guidance can empower you to identify and harness your strengths, cultivate self-compassion, and build a solid foundation for your emotional well-being.

Importantly, therapy or counseling provides a confidential space where you can share your deepest concerns without fear of judgment or repercussions. It allows you to explore sensitive topics and unresolved emotions that may be challenging to discuss with friends or family. By engaging in a therapeutic relationship, you create an alliance with a trusted professional who is dedicated to your growth, healing, and personal development.

Remember that seeking the support of a therapist or counselor does not indicate weakness; rather, it reflects your commitment to self-care. It can accelerate your healing process and provide you with the tools and support necessary to rebuild your life with resilience and newfound emotional well-being.

Here are some steps you can take to seek professional help when going through a divorce:

- **Find a qualified professional:** Look for a licensed therapist or counselor who specializes in divorce or relationship issues. You can ask for recommendations from friends or family, or search online for professionals in your area.

- **Schedule an initial consultation:** Many therapists offer a free initial consultation, which gives you a chance to meet with them and see if you feel comfortable working with them.

- **Be open and honest:** Be open and honest with your therapist about what you're going through and how you're feeling. Don't be afraid to ask questions and let them know what you hope to get out of therapy.

- **Follow through with treatment:** Commit to attending regular therapy sessions and following through with any homework or self-care practices your therapist recommends.

- **Consider group therapy:** Group therapy can be a helpful option for those going through a divorce, as it provides a supportive environment with others who are going through similar experiences.

- **Don't be afraid to switch therapists or coaches:** If you don't feel comfortable working with a therapist, it's okay to switch to someone else. It's important to find a therapist who you feel comfortable talking to and who can provide the support and guidance you need.

Practice Mindfulness

Mindfulness is a powerful tool for managing your emotions. By actively cultivating mindfulness, you can unlock a profound sense of inner calm, balance, and clarity.

To embark on the journey of mindfulness, begin by embracing complete presence in the here and now. Immerse yourself fully in the current moment, acknowledging both the external environment and the internal landscape of your thoughts and emotions. By anchoring your awareness in the present, you cultivate a deeper connection with your experiences, fostering a heightened sense of self-awareness.

As you practice mindfulness, adopt a non-judgmental perspective. Instead of labeling your thoughts and emotions as "good" or "bad," simply observe them with curiosity and acceptance. Cultivate a compassionate attitude towards yourself, acknowledging that emotions are natural and ever-changing aspects of the human experience. By refraining from passing judgment, you create a safe space for your emotions to arise and dissipate without resistance.

By consistently engaging in mindfulness, you gain a valuable vantage point from which to observe your thoughts and emotions. This heightened perspective allows you to recognize the transient nature of your feelings, preventing them from overwhelming you. Instead of being carried away by the intensity of your emotions, you can step back and view them from a more objective standpoint.

Moreover, mindfulness empowers you to respond skillfully to your emotions rather than reacting impulsively. By creating a mindful pause between a triggering event and your response, you can consciously choose how to act. This deliberate pause offers you the opportunity to consider alternative perspectives, assess the best course of action, and navigate challenging situations with greater clarity and composure.

Through mindfulness, you develop an intimate relationship with your inner world, nurturing self-compassion and self-understanding. It allows you to cultivate a deep sense of acceptance, acknowledging that all emotions, whether pleasant or unpleasant, are part of the human experience. By embracing them without resistance, you create space for personal growth, resilience, and emotional well-being.

Mindfulness serves as a powerful tool for managing your emotions. By embracing complete presence in the moment and adopting a non-judgmental perspective, you can gain valuable insights, minimize feelings of overwhelm, and navigate the complexities of your emotional landscape with grace. By incorporating mindfulness into your daily life, you embark on a transformative journey toward greater self-awareness, inner peace, and emotional balance.

Here are some tips on how to practice mindfulness when going through a divorce:

- **Focus on the present moment:** Mindfulness is about focusing on the present moment and paying attention to what's happening right now, rather than dwelling on the past or worrying about the future.

- **Use your breath as an anchor:** One way to stay present is to use your breath as an anchor. Take a few deep breaths and focus on the sensation of the breath moving in and out of your body.

- **Notice your thoughts and emotions:** Mindfulness involves observing your thoughts and emotions without judgment. Notice when your mind starts to wander or when difficult emotions arise and simply observe them without trying to push them away or get caught up in them.

- **Consider a consistent mindfulness practice:** Consider incorporating a mindfulness practice into your daily routine, such as through meditation, yoga, or a mindful walk in nature. These practices can help you stay grounded and centered during a difficult time.

Remember that mindfulness takes time and practice, so be patient with yourself and don't get discouraged if it feels challenging at first. With time and practice, mindfulness can become a helpful tool for coping with the emotions and stress of going through a divorce.

Reframe Negative Thoughts

It's easy to fall into negative thinking patterns after a divorce. Try to reframe negative thoughts by focusing on positive aspects of your life, such as your strengths, accomplishments, or opportunities for growth.

Following a divorce, it is natural to find oneself susceptible to negative thinking patterns that can hinder emotional well-being and personal growth. However, it is possible to reframe these negative thoughts and cultivate a more positive mindset. By consciously shifting your focus towards the positive aspects of your life, you can foster resilience and embrace a more optimistic outlook.

Acknowledging that negative thinking patterns can be a common response to the challenges of divorce is an important first step. Recognize that these thoughts may arise due to the emotional upheaval and adjustments that come with the end of a significant relationship. By understanding the origin of negative thoughts, you can take control of them and redirect your mental energy towards more constructive perspectives.

To reframe negative thoughts, consciously focus on the positive elements of your life. Take inventory of your strengths, talents, and qualities that make you unique. Reflect on past accomplishments and moments of personal growth that have shaped your journey. By directing your attention to these positive aspects, you can counterbalance the negativity and regain confidence and self-worth.

Additionally, embrace the notion that every experience, including divorce, presents opportunities for growth and personal development. Shift your perspective to view the challenges you face as potential catalysts for positive change. Explore how this transition can lead you to discover new passions, relationships, or a deeper understanding of yourself. Embrace the idea that you have the power to shape your future and create a fulfilling life beyond divorce.

Practicing gratitude can also be a powerful tool in reframing negative thoughts. Take time each day to identify and appreciate the things you are grateful for, whether they are simple pleasures or significant blessings. Focusing on gratitude can shift your attention away from negativity and foster contentment and hope.

Engaging in positive self-talk is another effective strategy. Replace self-critical or pessimistic thoughts with compassionate and empowering statements. Encourage yourself with affirmations that highlight your resilience, potential, and capacity to overcome challenges. By nurturing a positive internal dialogue, you can gradually rewire your thinking patterns and cultivate a more optimistic and self-affirming mindset.

Surrounding yourself with a supportive network of friends, family, or a professional support system will also help with this, in addition to the other advantages of seeking support that I've previously highlighted. Seek out individuals who uplift and encourage you, providing a fresh perspective and reminding you of your worth and potential. Engaging in open and honest conversations with trusted individuals can offer valuable insights and help you challenge and reframe negative thoughts.

Remember, reframing negative thoughts is a gradual process that requires patience and self-compassion. It may take time and consistent effort to reshape your thinking patterns. Be gentle with yourself along the way and celebrate small victories. By consciously shifting your focus towards the positive aspects of your life, embracing growth opportunities, and fostering a supportive environment, you can reframe negative thoughts and cultivate a more positive and resilient mindset in the aftermath of a divorce.

Here are some tips on how to reframe negative thoughts when going through a divorce:

- **Practice self-awareness:** Start by noticing your negative thoughts and the patterns they follow. Write them down and then take a step back to examine them.

- **Challenge negative thoughts:** Once you have identified negative thoughts, challenge them by asking yourself if they are true. Consider whether you're making assumptions or jumping to conclusions.

- **Look for evidence to the contrary:** If you're having trouble challenging negative thoughts, look for evidence to the contrary. For example, if you're thinking "I'll never find love again," remind yourself of times when you were happy and fulfilled without a partner.

- **Reframe negative thoughts:** Try to reframe negative thoughts into more positive or neutral ones. For example, instead of "I'm a failure because my marriage ended," try "Divorce is a difficult experience, but I am learning and growing from it."

- **Practice gratitude:** Focusing on things you're grateful for can help reframe negative thoughts. Each day, make a list of three things you're grateful for, no matter how small they may seem.

- **Seek support:** Reach out to friends and family members and consider talking to a therapist or counselor if you're struggling to reframe negative thoughts.

Remember that reframing negative thoughts takes time and practice, but it can be a powerful tool for coping with the emotions and stress of going through a divorce. With patience and persistence, you can learn to reframe negative thoughts and find a more positive and hopeful outlook.

Set Boundaries

Boundaries after a divorce are the limits and guidelines established to manage interactions and responsibilities between former partners in a way that promotes respect, reduces conflict, and ensures personal well-being. They help create a framework for handling communication, financial matters, parenting, and personal space in a manner that supports a healthy and functional post-divorce relationship.

What boundaries are:

- **Clear Guidelines:** Specific rules and expectations for interactions, communication, and responsibilities to prevent misunderstandings and reduce conflict.

- **Respectful Limits:** Measures to maintain personal space, privacy, and emotional well-being, ensuring that both parties' needs are acknowledged and respected.

- **Structured Agreements:** Predefined arrangements regarding financial obligations, co-parenting responsibilities, and social interactions to provide stability and predictability.

What boundaries are not:

- **Control Mechanisms:** Boundaries are not about controlling or dictating the other person's actions but about setting limits that help manage interactions and responsibilities constructively.

- **Permanent Barriers:** Boundaries are not rigid and unchangeable; they can be adjusted as circumstances evolve and as both parties work together to address new situations or concerns.

- **Forms of Punishment:** Boundaries are not meant to be punitive tools but rather frameworks to create a respectful and manageable post-divorce dynamic.

Setting Boundaries

Setting boundaries is the act of clearly defining and asserting your limits to protect your emotional, mental, and physical well-being. It is the courageous decision to prioritize your needs and values, refusing to tolerate anything that compromises your peace or self-respect. Boundaries empower you to take control of your life, build healthier relationships, and honor your worth, without guilt or hesitation. Examples:

- **Communication Boundaries:** Deciding to only communicate with your ex about necessary matters, such as children's schedules or financial arrangements, and avoiding personal or emotional conversations that could lead to conflict or manipulation.

- **Emotional Boundaries:** Refusing to engage in any emotional manipulation or guilt trips from your ex. This might involve stepping back from heated arguments or recognizing when they are trying to provoke an emotional response.

- **Time Boundaries:** Protecting your personal time and space. For example, only agreeing to meet with your ex for child-related matters during designated times and making sure to keep your personal time free for self-care or other priorities.

- **Physical Boundaries:** Ensuring that your personal space is respected. This could mean keeping physical distance at meetings or transitions or not allowing them to enter your home without permission.

- **Financial Boundaries:** Establishing clear expectations about financial responsibilities post-divorce, whether it's child support, alimony, or shared expenses, and sticking to agreed-upon terms to avoid further financial strain or disputes.

- **Social Boundaries:** You have the right to set social boundaries after divorce. This includes choosing who you spend time with, what personal details you share, and how you engage on social media to maintain your privacy and well-being.

Setting these boundaries helps you maintain control over your life, protect your well-being, and move forward with clarity and confidence in your new chapter.

Recognize that setting boundaries is a sign of self-respect and self-care. It allows you to establish limits on what is acceptable to you and to protect your emotional well-being. It's crucial to identify your personal boundaries by reflecting on your needs, values, and limits. Consider what behaviors, conversations, or interactions are uncomfortable or trigger negative emotions for you.

Once you have a clear understanding of your boundaries, express your needs, expectations, and limits respectfully, using "I" statements to avoid sounding accusatory or confrontational. Articulate your boundaries with clarity and firmness, emphasizing the importance of mutual respect and understanding in maintaining a healthy post-divorce relationship.

Setting boundaries in divorce involves more than just navigating your relationship with your ex—it's about asserting your needs with *everyone* involved in your life during this time of transition. This could mean setting boundaries:

- **With Your Ex-Spouse**: Clearly defining what is acceptable in your interactions, such as only discussing child-related matters and avoiding personal or emotional conversations. It's about protecting yourself from unnecessary conflict while still maintaining a civil relationship for co-parenting.

- **With Family**: Setting boundaries with well-meaning family members who might offer unsolicited advice or take sides in the divorce. You can politely explain that while you appreciate their concern, certain topics are off-limits, or you need time to process things privately.

- **With Friends**: Sometimes, friends may unintentionally cross boundaries by asking probing questions about your divorce or offering advice that doesn't align with your goals. You can kindly express that while you value their support, there are limits to what you wish to discuss, or you may need space to figure things out on your own.

Once you've clarified your boundaries, it's important to communicate them respectfully. Use "I" statements to express your needs, like "I need some time to myself after work" or "I prefer not to discuss personal matters in front of the children." This approach minimizes defensiveness and keeps the conversation focused on your feelings and requirements.

By articulating your boundaries with clarity, consistency, and firmness, you reinforce the importance of mutual respect in maintaining healthy relationships—whether that's with your ex, your family, or friends—after the divorce.

I've already gone through some examples of boundaries you can set with your ex-spouse. Here are examples of setting boundaries with family and friends:

With Family:

- **Privacy Respect:** Request that family members respect your boundaries and avoid prying into personal matters or divorce details, maintaining your privacy and emotional space.

- **Support Limits:** Clearly communicate how much support you need and in what form and establish limits to avoid overreliance or misunderstanding.

Coping with the Emotional Fallout

- **Conflict Handling:** Set guidelines for how family members should address or discuss any issues related to the divorce, ensuring that their support is constructive rather than exacerbating conflicts.

With Friends:

- **Emotional Boundaries:** Let friends know how much you wish to discuss the divorce and set limits on conversations to avoid feeling overwhelmed by constant discussions.

- **Social Boundaries:** Establish clear expectations for how friends should navigate interactions with your ex or manage social events where both you and your ex might be present.

- **Support Role:** Define what kind of support you value from friends, such as practical help or emotional encouragement, and set boundaries to avoid misunderstandings or feeling pressured.

By approaching the conversation from a place of emotional stability, you increase the likelihood of your boundaries being understood and respected. Avoid becoming defensive or engaging in arguments, as this can escalate conflicts and hinder effective communication.

Consistency is key to maintaining boundaries. Continually reinforce and uphold your boundaries, even if they are initially met with resistance or pushback. Be prepared for potential challenges, and stand firm in your commitment to your emotional well-being. It's natural for others to test or question your boundaries, but staying true to yourself and your needs is vital for your overall emotional health.

Remember that setting boundaries during a divorce is a mutual process. While it's essential to establish and assert your own boundaries, it is just as important to respect the boundaries set by others. Foster open and honest communication to ensure that all parties involved have the space they need to navigate the transition effectively. By fostering an environment of mutual respect and understanding, you can cultivate healthier and more harmonious relationships.

Setting boundaries may involve making difficult decisions and enforcing consequences when necessary. Be prepared to follow through with the consequences you have communicated, even if it feels challenging. This demonstrates your commitment to self-care and reinforces the importance of respecting your boundaries.

Here are some tips on how to set boundaries:

- **Identify your boundaries:** Start by identifying your boundaries. Think about what you are willing and unwilling to accept in terms of communication, behavior, and interactions with your ex-spouse, family, or friends.

- **Communicate your boundaries clearly:** Be specific about what you will and will not tolerate.

- **Stick to your boundaries**: It's important to stick to your boundaries, even if it's difficult or uncomfortable. Consistency is key when it comes to setting boundaries.

It can be beneficial to seek support from a therapist or counselor who can assist you in establishing and maintaining healthy boundaries with your ex-spouse, family, and friends. It's also important to be flexible and willing to negotiate when setting boundaries. Listen to the other person's perspective and be open to finding a compromise that works for both of you.

Here are some examples:

- **Co-Parenting Schedule:** If both parents have different preferences for the children's schedule, a compromise might involve creating a balanced co-parenting plan that includes flexible visitation times and ensures both parents have meaningful time with the children.

- **Financial Responsibilities:** When dividing financial obligations, such as child support or shared expenses, a compromise might involve negotiating a fair split of costs that reflects each party's financial situation and agreed-upon responsibilities.

- **Communication Methods:** If one party prefers regular updates while the other prefers less frequent communication, a compromise could be establishing scheduled times for discussions or using a co-parenting app to manage communication efficiently.

- **Social Events:** If both parties have concerns about attending social events where the other will be present, a compromise might involve agreeing on neutral venues or splitting attendance at events to minimize discomfort.

- **Parenting Decisions:** When there are disagreements about parenting styles or decisions, a compromise could involve creating a set of shared guidelines that respect both parents' approaches and focus on the children's best interests.

- **Personal Space:** If there are conflicts over personal boundaries, such as how much time one person spends in shared spaces or the level of involvement in each other's lives, a compromise might involve clear agreements on respecting personal space and privacy.

- **Holiday Arrangements:** When it comes to holiday celebrations, a compromise might involve alternating holidays or finding a way to celebrate together in a manner that respects both parties' traditions and preferences.

- **Support and Involvement:** If one party feels unsupported in their role, a compromise might involve specific agreements on how each person will contribute or participate in shared responsibilities or events.

Setting boundaries can help you manage your emotions and reduce conflict when going through a divorce. With patience and persistence, you can learn to set and enforce healthy boundaries that help you navigate this difficult time.

How I Reclaimed My Identity After Divorce

Divorce is more than just the end of a marriage—it's the unraveling of an identity that had been intertwined with someone else's. When I walked away from my marriage, I wasn't just leaving behind a relationship; I was stepping into an unfamiliar world where I had to redefine who I was outside of being a spouse. It was both terrifying and liberating.

Losing Myself in the Marriage

Looking back, I realize how much of myself I had lost over the years. I had molded parts of my personality, my dreams, and even my daily routines around my ex-partner. The hobbies I once loved faded into the background. The goals I had set for myself before marriage felt distant, buried under the responsibilities of being a wife and, eventually, a mother.

At first, I didn't even recognize how much I had changed. I told myself it was normal to compromise, to adjust, to shift my priorities for the sake of the marriage. But when the relationship ended, I was left standing in the wreckage, wondering, "Who am I now?"

The Journey Back to Myself

Reclaiming my identity wasn't an instant process—it was a journey of self-discovery, one step at a time. At first, I felt lost, unsure of where to even begin. But slowly, I started peeling back the layers, rediscovering the woman I had been before marriage—and the person I was meant to become.

Reconnecting with My Passions
One of the first things I did was revisit the hobbies and interests I had set aside. I started journaling again, pouring out my thoughts onto the pages, using writing as a way to heal. I spent time in nature, going for walks and even starting a garden with my children. We created the most beautiful rose garden in the neighborhood, a small but powerful reminder that beauty can grow from struggle.

Rediscovering My Independence
For years, I had made decisions as part of a couple. Now, I had to relearn how to trust myself. The first time I made a major decision on my own, I felt uncertain. But with each choice—big or small—I gained confidence. I realized that I was capable, strong, and resourceful.

Setting New Goals
With my marriage behind me, I had the opportunity to dream again. What did I want for myself? Where did I see my future going? I sat down and made a list of personal and professional goals—some small, some ambitious. Slowly, I started working toward them, proving to myself that life wasn't just about survival—it was about growth.

Surrounding Myself with the Right People

Not everyone understood my journey. Some friends drifted away, unable to relate to my new reality. But I also found new connections—people who encouraged me, who reminded me of my worth, who didn't define me by my past. I learned that the relationships I chose to keep had to be ones that lifted me up, not ones that kept me stuck.

Redefining My Self-Worth

One of the biggest shifts I made was learning to value myself outside of my roles as a wife or mother. My worth wasn't tied to my marital status, my financial situation, or my past mistakes. It was rooted in who I was as a person—the love I gave, the strength I carried, and the resilience I built through every hardship.

How *You* Can Reclaim *Your* Identity

If you are going through a similar journey, know that you are not alone. Here are some steps you can take to reclaim your identity after divorce:

- ☑ Explore What Makes You Happy – Take time to revisit old hobbies or try new ones. Whether it's painting, reading, traveling, or learning something new, give yourself the space to rediscover what brings you joy.

- ☑ Make Decisions for Yourself – Start small, like choosing how to spend your weekend, and work up to bigger decisions. The more you trust yourself, the stronger your confidence will become.

- ☑ Set Goals for Your Future – Write down things you want to accomplish, no matter how big or small. Having a vision for your future can help guide you toward a fulfilling new chapter.

- ☑ Surround Yourself with Supportive People – Find a support system of friends, family, or even a therapist who uplift you and encourage your growth.

- ☑ Define Your Own Worth – Remember, your value isn't defined by your past relationship. Focus on the qualities that make you unique and embrace the person you are becoming.

Embracing Your New Identity

Reclaiming my identity after divorce wasn't just about rediscovering who I used to be—it was about stepping into a new, stronger version of myself. The woman who emerged from this process wasn't just surviving; she was thriving. She had learned to stand on her own, to trust herself, and to embrace the future with open arms.

Divorce may have closed one chapter, but it didn't define my entire story. In fact, it gave me the chance to write a new one—one where I was the main character, fully in control of my own narrative. And that, I realized, was the greatest gift of all.

If you're on this journey too, take your time. Explore what makes you happy. Surround yourself with people who uplift you. And most importantly, believe in yourself. Your identity isn't gone—it's just waiting to be rediscovered.

Examples of ways to implement consequences in various situations following a divorce:

1. Unmet Communication Expectations
- **Example**: If your ex-partner repeatedly fails to communicate regarding important matters about the children or legal arrangements, you can establish a clear consequence, like limiting communication to written forms only (email or text), or only discussing the children in specific time slots.

- **How to Enforce**: "Since we've agreed that we need better communication, I will no longer discuss the children over the phone, and any further communications will be done via email only."

2. Respecting Personal Space and Time
- **Example**: If someone, such as an ex, continues to show up uninvited to your home or disrupts your personal time, you may set a boundary with clear consequences, like no longer allowing them in without prior permission or limiting the duration of their visits.

- **How to Enforce**: "If you come to my house unannounced again, I will not be opening the door. Please call or text first to make sure it's a good time."

3. Inconsistent Financial Contributions

- **Example**: If an ex-spouse continues to miss financial obligations like child support or alimony, a consequence might be notifying them that you will be contacting legal authorities or seeking mediation.

- **How to Enforce**: "I've noticed that the payment has been late again, and if this continues, I will need to bring this matter to court to ensure regular payments."

4. Unhealthy Social Interactions

- **Example**: If a family member or friend constantly makes negative remarks about your new life or relationship, you might need to enforce a consequence by limiting your interactions with them or setting boundaries on the topics of conversation.

- **How to Enforce**: "If you continue to criticize my decisions, I will have to stop speaking with you about my personal life. Please respect my choices or I will take a step back from our relationship."

5. Disrespecting Boundaries in New Relationships

- **Example**: If an ex or acquaintance tries to make unwanted advances or disrespect personal boundaries, the consequence could be clear communication about the end of the relationship or a definitive statement on the direction of your relationship with them.

- **How to Enforce**: "If the boundaries I've set are not respected, I will have to completely end all contact with you. It's important to me that we both move forward with mutual respect."

6. Failure to Adhere to Agreements Regarding Child Custody Due to Unclear or Nonexistent Terms

- **Example**: If an ex consistently fails to adhere to child custody arrangements, you can reinforce the consequences by stating that you will document the occurrences and take legal action if necessary.

- **How to Enforce**: "If the custody schedule isn't followed again, I will need to consult with my attorney to review the agreement and ensure it is properly enforced."

7. Chronic Neglect of Important Decisions

- **Example**: If your ex fails to contribute to or participate in decisions about the children's education or medical care, the consequence might be taking on the decision-making responsibility yourself or seeking joint custody clarification.

- **How to Enforce**: "If you continue to neglect your responsibilities in making decisions for the kids, I will be forced to take full responsibility for those decisions on my own."

8. Violating Parenting Rules or Agreements

- **Example**: If your ex-partner violates agreed-upon rules for the children, such as allowing them to break curfew, you can set consequences like restricting visitation times or ensuring that all future visits are supervised.

- **How to Enforce**: "If the children's curfew is not respected again, we will have to revisit the visitation schedule, and I will require supervision during visits."

By enforcing consequences consistently and with clarity, you're not only protecting your own well-being but also modeling healthy boundaries and accountability for your children and others involved in your life. These examples allow you to set firm but fair limits that encourage respect and cooperation, helping you move forward confidently in your post-divorce life.

Anger

Anger is a natural and common response to the loss and changes that come with divorce. It can be directed at the ex-partner, oneself, or even at others who are not directly involved. Understanding and effectively coping with anger is essential for navigating the emotional challenges of divorce.

Firstly, it's important to acknowledge that anger is a valid and normal response to the upheaval you're going through. Allow yourself to recognize and accept this emotion without judgment. It indicates that something significant has occurred and that you are processing the associated feelings of hurt, betrayal, or disappointment. Validating your anger allows you to give it the attention it deserves, facilitating a healthier approach to managing it.

Finding healthy and constructive ways to express your anger is key. One effective method is through journaling. Grab a pen and paper, and let your emotions flow onto the pages. Write about what you're feeling, why you're angry, and the impact the divorce has had on your life. The act of writing can be cathartic and provide a safe outlet for releasing pent-up emotions.

I've mentioned this before because it's truly valuable advice for any situation: Seeking support from a therapist or a trusted friend can be a game-changer. Whether you're navigating personal challenges or just need someone to talk to, having the guidance of a professional or the reassurance of a supportive friend can make a significant difference. They can offer insights, emotional support, and practical strategies that help you cope more effectively and find your way through difficult times. Engaging in physical activity can also be an effective outlet for anger. Exercise provides an opportunity to release pent-up energy and tension while promoting overall well-being. Engage in activities that resonate with you, such as running, swimming, practicing yoga, or participating in martial arts. Mindfulness practices, once again, play a crucial role in coping with anger as they offer effective tools for managing and transforming this intense emotion. By incorporating mindfulness into your coping strategies, you can cultivate a greater sense of self-awareness and develop healthier responses to anger.

By bringing your attention to the present moment, you create space to acknowledge and accept your anger, rather than being consumed by it. Mindfulness helps you develop a deeper understanding of the triggers and underlying causes of your anger, empowering you to respond to it with more compassion.

One mindfulness technique that can be particularly helpful in coping with anger is mindful breathing. Taking slow, deep breaths and focusing your attention on the sensation of each inhale and exhale helps anchor you in the present moment. This simple practice provides a moment of pause and allows you to regain a sense of calmness and clarity when anger arises. Through mindful breathing, you can create a space between the anger and your response, enabling you to choose a more skillful and constructive reaction.

Another mindfulness practice that supports anger management is body scan meditation. This involves systematically directing your attention to different parts of your body and noticing any tension, discomfort, or other sensations. By scanning your body with curiosity and non-judgment, you can become aware of physical manifestations of anger, such as tightness in the chest or clenched fists. This awareness helps you release physical tension and become more attuned to your body's signals, providing an opportunity to respond to anger with greater self-compassion and self-regulation.

In addition to these specific mindfulness techniques, the overall practice of mindfulness encourages an attitude of acceptance and non-reactivity towards anger. Rather than suppressing or avoiding anger, mindfulness invites you to acknowledge it with kindness and curiosity. By allowing anger to arise and pass without judgment, you can develop a more balanced and compassionate relationship with this challenging emotion.

Regular mindfulness practice creates a foundation of self-awareness and emotional resilience, which supports long-term anger management. As you integrate mindfulness into your daily life, you may find that you become more attuned to early signs of anger, allowing you to intervene before it escalates. Mindfulness also fosters a mindset of openness, flexibility, and adaptability, enabling you to navigate conflicts and difficult emotions with greater clarity and equanimity.

It's important to note that mindfulness is not a quick-fix solution to anger. But by dedicating time each day to cultivate mindfulness, whether formally or informally, you can gradually strengthen your ability to cope with anger and respond to it in more skillful and constructive ways.

It's important to remember that managing anger is an ongoing process. It may take time to develop healthier responses to this emotion, and setbacks may occur along the way. Be patient with yourself and practice self-compassion as you navigate through this journey of healing. Celebrate the progress you make in expressing and managing your anger in healthy ways, no matter how small.

Here are some tips on how to handle anger when going through a divorce:

Acknowledge your anger: The first step in handling anger is to acknowledge and accept that you're feeling it. Don't try to suppress or ignore your anger, as this can lead to more intense and prolonged feelings of anger.

If you're feeling angry, take a step back and ask yourself—what's really causing it? Are you mad at your ex, frustrated with yourself, or just overwhelmed by everything that's happened? Sometimes, anger is just the surface emotion, but underneath it, there's hurt, disappointment, or even fear.

For example, when I went through my divorce, I would catch myself getting angry over small things—like a late text response or a change in plans. But when I really sat with it, I realized I wasn't just mad about those moments; I was grieving the loss of control over a life I had planned. Once I understood that, I could start dealing with the real emotions instead of just reacting in anger.

So, next time you feel that frustration building, pause and ask yourself—what's beneath this anger? When you can name it, you can start working through it in a way that actually helps you heal.

Practice relaxation techniques: Anger can be a physically and emotionally taxing experience. Practice relaxation techniques such as deep breathing, meditation, or yoga to help calm your body and mind.

Consider forgiveness: Forgiveness can be a powerful tool for letting go of anger and resentment. While it may be difficult, consider whether forgiveness is a possibility for you and work on letting go of grudges and resentments.

Be patient with yourself and stay persistent. With effort, you can learn to manage your anger in healthy ways and move forward with your life.

Sadness

Like anger, sadness is a natural and expected emotion that often accompanies divorce. It arises from the sense of loss, grief, and adjustment to the end of a significant relationship. Coping with sadness requires acknowledging and honoring these emotions rather than suppressing or denying them. By allowing yourself to fully experience and process your sadness, you can begin the healing process.

One important aspect of coping with sadness is giving yourself permission to feel the emotions. Understand that sadness is a normal response to a major life change, and that it's okay to feel sad. Avoid judging or criticizing yourself for experiencing these emotions. Instead, offer yourself compassion and understanding, recognizing that your feelings are valid.

Engaging in activities that bring joy or comfort can be beneficial in managing sadness. Surrounding yourself with loved ones who provide support and understanding can provide comfort and connection during this challenging time. Spending quality time with family and friends, engaging in meaningful conversations or participating in enjoyable activities together, can help uplift your spirits and remind you of the positive aspects of your life.

Finding solace in solitary activities can also be helpful. Reading a book, listening to music, taking a walk in nature, or practicing mindfulness can provide moments of respite and allow for introspection. These activities can serve as healthy distractions and create a space for you to process your emotions at your own pace. It's important to remember that healing from sadness takes time and that there is no predetermined timeline for grief. Allow yourself to grieve and honor the process. Be patient and gentle with yourself, allowing the healing process to unfold naturally.

I know I've said this before, but sometimes, working with a therapist, coach, or counselor can be incredibly helpful when dealing with sadness. They provide a safe space to delve into your emotions, offer practical tools for managing them, and help you address any deeper issues related to the divorce. Therapy can also give you fresh perspectives and coping strategies to move forward.

In summary, sadness is a common emotion experienced after divorce, and it's important to allow yourself to feel and process these emotions.

Here are some tips on how to cope with sadness when going through a divorce:

Allow yourself to feel sad: Acknowledge that sadness is a normal part of the grieving process. Don't try to suppress your emotions or put on a brave face.

Take care of yourself: Taking care of yourself is important when coping with sadness. Get plenty of rest, eat a healthy diet, exercise, and spend time with loved ones. For me, taking care of my physical well-being has been a huge part of my healing journey. I've learned that movement isn't just about staying active—it's about feeling good in my own body again. Whether it's going for a walk, dancing around my living room, or doing a bit of yoga, I make an effort to move in ways that bring me joy. Exercise has helped me clear my mind, release stress, and boost my energy, even on days when I feel emotionally drained. I've realized that when I take care of my body, I'm also taking care of my heart and mind. If you're going through a tough time, find something physical that makes you feel good—it doesn't have to be intense, just something that helps you reconnect with yourself.

Be Kind to Yourself: Healing Takes Time

One of the most important things I learned during my journey was how to be gentle with myself. It's easy to be your own worst critic, wondering if you're handling things the "right" way or if you should be further along in your healing. But the truth is, there's no perfect timeline for moving forward.

I had days when I felt strong and confident, and then there were days when I could barely get out of bed. At first, I would beat myself up for feeling stuck or not having all the answers. But over time, I realized that healing isn't about getting everything right—it's about allowing yourself the space to feel, process, and grow.

So, if you're struggling, remind yourself that it's okay to have difficult moments. It's okay to not have all the answers right away. Talk to yourself the way you would comfort a friend—with patience, understanding, and kindness. The more you practice self-compassion, the more you'll begin to trust that you're exactly where you need to be on your journey.

While dealing with sadness after a divorce requires time and effort, remember that with support, self-care, and compassion for yourself, you can gradually heal and rebuild your life.

Guilt

Guilt is a prevalent and complex emotion that often comes with divorce, as individuals may find themselves questioning their actions or feeling responsible for the end of the relationship. It can manifest in various ways, such as feeling guilty for the role played in the breakup or for the impact the divorce may have on children or loved ones. Coping with guilt requires a compassionate and understanding approach towards oneself and a commitment to growth and healing.

One important step in coping with guilt is practicing self-compassion. Recognize that divorce is a challenging and multifaceted experience, and it is natural to have mixed emotions and doubts. Instead of being harsh and self-critical, offer yourself kindness and understanding. Remind yourself that you are human, and making mistakes is a part of life. Embrace self-forgiveness and let go of the burden of guilt that may be weighing you down.

It can also be helpful to reframe your perspective on guilt. Instead of dwelling on the negative aspects, try to find lessons and opportunities for growth. Reflect on the events that led to the divorce and identify areas where personal growth can occur. Use this as an opportunity for self-reflection and self-improvement. By focusing on personal growth, you can shift your energy towards positive change rather than being consumed by guilt.

Engaging in acts of kindness or volunteer work can be a powerful way to alleviate feelings of guilt and regain a sense of purpose. By extending compassion and support to others, you redirect your focus towards helping and making a positive impact. Volunteering in organizations or causes that resonate with your values can provide a sense of fulfillment and help you regain your self-worth. Through these acts of kindness, you may also gain perspective and realize that everyone faces challenges in life, and you are not alone in experiencing difficult emotions.

It's essential to remember that healing from guilt takes time and that it is a deeply personal journey. Be patient with yourself and allow yourself to go through the process of self-forgiveness and growth. Surround yourself with a supportive network of family and friends who can provide encouragement and understanding along the way. Navigating guilt requires self-compassion, reframing perspectives, engaging in acts of kindness, and, often, seeking professional support. Embrace self-forgiveness, recognize the opportunities for growth, and channel your energy towards positive changes. By practicing self-compassion, focusing on personal growth, and seeking support, you can gradually release the burden of guilt.

In this chapter, we've explored some common reasons why you might feel guilty during or after a divorce, such as self-blame for the end of your marriage, concerns about the impact on your children, the pressure of letting down others, and the discomfort of breaking societal norms. These feelings are a natural part of the divorce process, but they can be overwhelming.

To help you navigate these emotions, we've discussed practical strategies to cope with guilt. Practicing self-compassion, focusing on positive aspects of your life, seeking support from a therapist, taking responsibility for your actions, and working towards self-forgiveness are all essential steps in addressing and managing these feelings.

As you move forward, it's important to understand that dealing with guilt is a process that takes time and effort. Embracing these strategies can support your journey towards healing and self-acceptance. In the next chapter, we'll delve into building resilience and embracing personal growth, focusing on how to transform the challenges of divorce into opportunities for self-improvement and new beginnings.

CHAPTER TWO

Reinventing Your Identity

After a divorce, the process of redefining yourself and creating a new identity is an important step towards healing and moving forward.

Divorce can deeply impact your sense of identity, leaving you feeling uncertain about who you are and where you fit in the world. Despite the upheaval, it also opens up a valuable opportunity for self-discovery and personal growth. Rebuilding your identity after a divorce is not just about adapting to change but also about embracing it as a chance to redefine yourself. This process can be empowering and transformative, allowing you to forge a new path and create a fulfilling chapter in your life. By exploring new interests, setting fresh goals, and understanding yourself better, you can turn this challenging time into a period of significant personal development and renewal.

Reinventing your identity after a divorce is an empowering experience. It's a time of self-discovery, growth, and personal transformation that allows you to define yourself on your own terms and build a future that aligns with your true desires and aspirations.

One of the most significant aspects of this journey is reclaiming your autonomy and rediscovering who you are as an individual. Divorce often involves the dissolution of shared dreams, roles, and expectations, and it can leave you feeling lost or disconnected from your sense of self. However, it also opens up a world of possibilities to rediscover your passions, interests, and personal values.

Reinventing Your Identity

During this process, you have the freedom to explore your authentic self and make choices that resonate with your newfound independence. You can reflect on your core values and make intentional decisions that align with who you are and what you want for your life. This may involve reevaluating your priorities, setting new goals, and pursuing activities that bring you joy and fulfillment.

Reinventing your identity after a divorce also means embracing personal growth and self-improvement. It's an opportunity to confront any limiting beliefs or self-doubt that may have held you back in the past and to cultivate a mindset of resilience, strength, and self-confidence. As you embark on this journey, you may discover hidden strengths and talents that you didn't realize you had, allowing you to tap into your full potential.

Creating a new chapter in your life after divorce requires courage to let go of old patterns, relationships, and beliefs that no longer serve you. By embracing change, you open yourself up to new opportunities, experiences, and connections.

Above all, reinventing your identity after a divorce is about finding your own sense of fulfillment and happiness. It's about embracing your individuality and creating a life that reflects your true desires and values. By taking charge of your own narrative, you can shape a future that is filled with purpose, authenticity, and joy.

Remember, this process is unique to you, and there is no set timeline for reinventing your identity. It may take time to explore different aspects of yourself and to fully embrace the changes ahead. Be patient, kind, and compassionate with yourself as you navigate this transformative journey.

Redefining yourself after a divorce can be challenging, but it is a crucial step in moving forward and building a fulfilling life.

Let Go of Old Roles

After a divorce, it can be difficult to let go of the roles and identities that were associated with the relationship, such as being a spouse or partner. To redefine yourself, it is important to let go of these old roles and the expectations that came with them. This may involve rethinking one's values, goals, and priorities and reframing them to align with the current life circumstances. To begin, it's important to reflect on the roles and expectations that were part of your previous relationship. These roles might have included being a spouse, a partner, or even a caretaker. Consider how these roles influenced your identity and shaped your actions and decisions. Acknowledge the emotions that arise as you let go of these roles, such as sadness, grief, or uncertainty, and allow yourself the space to process them.

Next, take the time to reevaluate your values, goals, and priorities. Are there any values that have shifted or evolved? Are there new goals or aspirations that you would like to pursue?

Reinventing Your Identity

Reframing your values, goals, and priorities involves aligning them with your current life circumstances. This may require a period of self-reflection and introspection. Consider the lessons you have learned from your past experiences and how they can inform your present and future. As you redefine yourself, be open to exploring new opportunities, interests, and passions that resonate with your authentic self.

Embracing change and being open to new possibilities is an important aspect of this process. Allow yourself to step outside of your comfort zone and be willing to try new things. This could involve exploring new hobbies, engaging in personal development activities, or seeking out new social connections. Embrace the freedom to shape your life based on your own desires and aspirations.

It's normal to encounter challenges and setbacks along the way, but these can serve as opportunities for further self-reflection and adjustment.

Connecting with others who have faced similar transitions can be incredibly supportive as you redefine yourself after divorce. By sharing your experiences with those who understand, you can find valuable insights and encouragement. In addition to joining support groups or community activities, you might also find it fulfilling to engage in volunteer work or connect with women who have experienced similar traumas. For me, leaning into my community and working with others who have been through similar challenges has provided both a sense of belonging and a source of strength. These interactions not only offer practical advice and emotional support but also help you feel more grounded and empowered as you navigate this transformative journey.

Reinventing Yourself After Divorce: Rediscovering Your Identity and Embracing New Possibilities

When you've spent years as part of a couple, losing that role can leave you questioning who you are and what you stand for. The transition from being "we" to being "I" can feel jarring, and suddenly, you may struggle with a sense of not existing in the way you once did. However, this loss of identity is not the end—it's an opportunity to reconnect with the essence of who you are as an individual.

The first step in this journey is to explore who you are outside of your former role. Take some time to reflect and list the qualities you value about yourself that are distinct from your role as a wife or partner. What are your personal strengths? What are the traits that make you unique? When do you feel most empowered or at your best? Identifying the aspects of yourself that have always been there—yet may have been overshadowed by your relationship—can serve as a powerful foundation as you begin the process of reinventing yourself.

Divorce doesn't just signify the end of a relationship; it marks a profound transformation in your sense of self. This period of reinvention is your chance to actively shape your identity, one that reflects the changes in your life and embraces the new possibilities that lie ahead. It's a time to rediscover parts

Reinventing Your Identity

of yourself that you may have overlooked or even forgotten about during the course of your marriage.

One of the most empowering ways to navigate this process is to explore new hobbies, interests, and passions. Engaging in activities that bring you joy and fulfillment can reignite parts of yourself that have been dormant for years. Whether it's taking up painting, learning to play an instrument, practicing yoga, or even traveling to new places, these activities can help you reconnect with your authentic self. They allow you to expand your horizons, nurture your creativity, and experience personal growth in ways that may have been impossible when you were entrenched in your previous role.

This period of reinvention is also a prime opportunity to evaluate your career and professional life. Divorce can be a wake-up call that prompts you to reassess whether your current job aligns with your passions, values, and aspirations. Perhaps there is a new career path you've always been curious about, or a new business idea you've dreamed of pursuing. Now is the time to explore those possibilities. Redirecting your focus toward a career that resonates with your true self can provide a profound sense of purpose and fulfillment that extends far beyond financial success.

As you embark on your journey of reinvention, surrounding yourself with the right people is essential. Building new relationships and expanding your social network will play a critical role in your self-discovery process. Seek out individuals who understand and support the changes you're going through. Surrounding yourself with people who support your reinvention can provide the confidence boost needed to pursue new opportunities and embrace the changes ahead.

Embracing new possibilities also means stepping outside your comfort zone. As you create new identities and roles for yourself, it's important to approach this process with openness and curiosity. Growth often comes when we venture into unfamiliar territory and face new challenges. Whether it's starting a new hobby, launching a new career, or meeting new people, allow yourself to embrace these experiences with patience and self-compassion. There will be moments of doubt and uncertainty, but remember that each step you take toward reinvention is a step closer to discovering the fullest version of yourself.

Through the process of redefining your identity, you will not only reshape how you see yourself, but also how the world sees you. Your reinvention allows you to build a new life that reflects your true potential and honors the person you are becoming. By embracing change with grace, courage, and determination, you can create a life that feels fulfilling, meaningful, and aligned with your deepest desires.

Identity and Self-Worth After Divorce: Rebuilding from Within

A major life transition like divorce can deeply affect one's sense of identity and self-worth. The emotional and practical implications of divorce can disrupt many aspects of your life, from your social circles and finances to your living

Reinventing Your Identity

arrangements and overall sense of purpose. In this upheaval, it's common for people to question who they are, what they stand for, and where they fit into the world now that their identity is no longer defined by the marriage.

The truth is that while divorce may shake your self-image, it doesn't define your worth. The process of rebuilding your self-worth and sense of identity after divorce involves both acknowledging the pain of the past and embracing the possibilities of the future. This is the time to affirm that you are more than your relationship status, more than your past, and more than the roles you once played.

Reinventing yourself is not about forgetting who you were but about rediscovering the parts of you that were always there, waiting to be nurtured. Through this process, you have the chance to build a life based on your own terms, one that reflects your strengths, passions, and aspirations. It's a powerful opportunity to reclaim control, rewrite your story, and move forward with a renewed sense of self-worth.

The road to reinvention isn't always easy, but by taking small, meaningful steps toward redefining who you are and what you want, you can build a life that's vibrant, fulfilling, and truly reflective of your authentic self.

Here are some ways that divorce can affect one's sense of identity and self-worth:

Divorce can be a profound experience that alters many aspects of your life, especially your sense of identity. For many people, their identity was deeply intertwined with their role as a spouse or partner. When that relationship ends, it can feel like you're losing a key part of who you are, and this loss can extend beyond just the relationship itself.

Take, for example, someone who had spent years developing close friendships with their spouse's family or friends. After the divorce, these relationships can become strained or even come to an end, creating a sense of isolation. You may no longer fit into the social circles or gatherings that were once a regular part of your life. Friends and family may feel uncomfortable or uncertain about how to relate to you now that your role as a partner has changed. This sense of disconnection can be especially painful if these relationships were an integral part of your identity.

Moreover, divorce can also lead to a feeling of disconnection from your broader community. If much of your social life was tied to your marriage, like attending events as a couple, or if your community support came from family-centered activities, you might suddenly feel like an outsider. This can be especially hard if the relationships within your community were primarily centered around the idea of you being part of a partnership. Without that role, it may seem like you no longer have a place within your social environment.

But while these feelings of loss are real and valid, it's important to recognize that you have the power to rebuild your social identity. This process starts by creating new connections that reflect who you are now, not just who you were. Seek out new social opportunities that align with your interests and passions.

Reinventing Your Identity

For example, you might join a book club, start volunteering for a cause you care about, or take up a hobby that has always interested you but was never possible during your marriage. Doing so can help you build new relationships and form a new sense of community that supports the person you are becoming.

Another critical aspect of reclaiming your identity after divorce is taking care of your own emotional well-being. This is a time to practice self-compassion and invest in your own growth. You may want to take up meditation or journaling to process your emotions or engage in activities that nourish your mental health. Seeking the guidance of a therapist or counselor during this time can also help you navigate the complex feelings that arise from the dissolution of your marriage, giving you tools to rebuild your self-worth and confidence.

It's important to remember that you are not defined solely by your role in a relationship. You have qualities, strengths, and passions that make you uniquely you. While divorce may shake your sense of self, it also provides an opportunity to rediscover who you are as an individual. Rebuilding your social identity and sense of belonging might take time, but it is a journey worth undertaking. By embracing new relationships, exploring new interests, and focusing on your well-being, you will gradually create a fulfilling and vibrant life that reflects your true self.

Financial Stress After Divorce: Coping with the Challenges

Divorce isn't just an emotional and social upheaval—it often comes with significant financial stress that can add an extra layer of pressure. Sorting out finances during a divorce can be overwhelming as you face the daunting task of dividing assets, dealing with legal fees, and figuring out how to support yourself independently. The financial implications of divorce can be far-reaching, affecting not only your immediate financial situation but also your long-term stability.

For many, divorce can mean a sudden shift in financial responsibility. If you were financially dependent on your spouse, the prospect of managing your own finances can feel especially daunting. You might need to make difficult decisions, such as selling personal belongings or taking on additional debt just to cover legal expenses and other costs associated with the divorce. These decisions can feel invasive, but they are often necessary steps to regain financial stability and independence.

The immediate impact of divorce on your finances is just the beginning. Over time, your lifestyle and standard of living may change. You may need to adjust to a smaller living space, a different budget, or new financial priorities. This adjustment can be particularly challenging if you were not the primary breadwinner in your marriage. Suddenly, you might find yourself facing the pressure of finding a new job or exploring different career paths to support yourself.

Reinventing Your Identity

If you were a stay-at-home parent or a homemaker, the prospect of entering or re-entering the workforce can be overwhelming. You may need to retrain, update your skills, or build up your confidence in a professional environment. These transitions are often stressful, but they are also opportunities for personal growth and empowerment. Remember that it is completely normal to feel uncertain and overwhelmed as you adjust to this new phase of life.

During this period, it's essential to take small steps to regain your financial footing. Consider working with a financial advisor who can help you navigate the division of assets, establish a budget, and create a plan for financial independence. You might also want to explore new career options that align with your skills and passions. There are often resources available, such as job training programs or networking opportunities, that can support you as you embark on this new financial chapter.

Most importantly, be patient with yourself. Financial stress after a divorce is a significant challenge, but it is not insurmountable. With time, planning, and support, you will find your footing and regain your financial independence. It's important to focus on rebuilding, step by step, and to remember that you are capable of thriving, even in the face of financial adversity. The road to financial stability after a divorce may take time, but with the right resources and mindset, you will find a way to create the life you deserve.

To cope with the financial impact of divorce, it's important to take steps to protect your financial well-being. This may include:

- Consulting with a financial advisor or planner to assess your financial situation and develop a plan for managing your finances post-divorce.

- Creating a budget that reflects your new financial situation and adjusting your lifestyle accordingly.

- Being proactive about managing your debt and working with creditors to develop a repayment plan.

- Seeking legal guidance to ensure that your assets and financial interests are protected during the divorce process.

- Exploring new career opportunities or seeking education or training to enhance your earning potential.

Remember that the financial impact of divorce can be challenging, but with careful planning and support, it's possible to regain financial stability and security.

Doubting your self-worth, especially after a major life event like divorce, is a completely natural and common experience. You are not alone in this. I, too, have had moments when my own sense of worth seemed to waver, and I questioned my value. There was a time when I doubted myself deeply, especially after I left an abusive relationship. The decision to leave was incredibly difficult, and even though the abuse was undeniable, I still found myself questioning if I should have stayed for the sake of the kids. I thought, "Maybe I

Reinventing Your Identity

could have made it work, maybe I could have endured for them." The guilt of leaving them in a broken home, even though I knew staying was harmful to me and them, was overwhelming.

Despite the abuse, part of me still held on to the belief that I could have done more, sacrificed more, and tried harder to keep the family intact. I feared that by leaving, I was doing something selfish, that I was letting my children down. But deep down, I knew that staying would have meant sacrificing my mental health and the well-being of all of us.

The truth was, I was trying to protect my children from an environment of constant emotional and physical harm. The strength it took to leave, to put my own safety and well-being first, was something I would later come to realize was the most loving thing I could do for them. But in those early moments, self-doubt clouded my thinking, making me question if I had made the right choice.

It was a long process, but eventually, I recognized that leaving wasn't just for me; it was for them too. The healthier I became, the better parent I could be. It took time to forgive myself, to accept that I had done what was necessary for our future. The self-doubt eventually faded as I found strength in my decision, realizing that sometimes, the hardest and most painful choices are the ones that lead us to a better life.

When my first book became a bestseller, I felt like I didn't deserve the success. As a writer, I had a moment of doubt after seeing my book climb the bestseller lists. I asked myself, "Do I deserve this? Am I really capable of helping others?" I had worked so hard and put so much of myself into the book, but a part of me still questioned my abilities and whether I was truly worthy of the recognition. However, I reminded myself that my experiences, my vulnerability, and my willingness to share them had resonated with others. The success was a reflection of my courage, and I had earned it.

Self-doubt is something we all experience. It doesn't define who we are or our potential for growth. Over time, I've learned that my self-worth isn't determined by external factors—it's something I get to define for myself. No matter what challenges or setbacks we face, we can always reconnect with our value and rise stronger.

Uncertainty about the future: Divorce can create uncertainty about the future, making it difficult to plan and set goals. During and after a divorce, people may experience a range of emotions and challenges that can make it hard to focus on their goals and aspirations. This can be due to factors such as changes in financial circumstances, custody arrangements, and social support systems.

To cope with the uncertainty of the future after a divorce, it can be helpful to focus on setting small, achievable goals. This can help create a sense of control and accomplishment, even in the face of uncertainty. Some strategies for setting goals during and after a divorce may include:

- **Making a list of short-term and long-term goals:** This can include anything from finding a new job to taking a trip or pursuing a new hobby.

- **Prioritizing goals:** Focus on the goals that are most important to you and that will have the biggest impact on your life.

- **Breaking goals down into manageable steps:** This can help make the goals feel more achievable and less overwhelming.

- **Celebrating successes:** Even small accomplishments can be a cause for celebration and can help boost your motivation and confidence.

Remember that the process of setting and achieving goals is a journey, and it's okay to experience setbacks and challenges along the way. By focusing on small, achievable goals and seeking support when needed, you can build a sense of hope and optimism for the future, even after a divorce.

Negative self-talk: Divorce can trigger negative self-talk and feelings of self-doubt and low self-esteem. It's common for people to experience negative thoughts and feelings about themselves during and after the process.

Negative self-talk can take many forms, such as self-blame, self-criticism, and self-doubt. It can be difficult to overcome these patterns of negative thinking, but some strategies may help:

- **Recognize and challenge negative thoughts:** Try to become more aware of your thoughts and challenge them when they are negative or unhelpful. Ask yourself if there is evidence to support these thoughts, and if not, try to reframe them into something more positive and realistic.

- **Focus on your strengths:** Identify your positive qualities and focus on them. Make a list of your strengths and accomplishments and read it regularly to remind yourself of your value and worth.

- **Take care of yourself:** Focus on your well-being by doing things that bring you joy and help you relax, like working out, meditating, or spending time with people who care about you.

- **Lean on others for support:** Open up to a trusted friend, family member, or therapist about what you're going through. They can listen and offer a fresh perspective, helping you navigate your feelings.

Remember that negative self-talk and feelings of low self-esteem are common during and after a divorce, but they do not define you. By practicing self-compassion, focusing on your strengths, and seeking support when needed, you can cultivate a more positive and resilient sense of self.

Changes in social support: Divorce often results in shifts in social support networks, which can feel both challenging and isolating. During and after a divorce, many people experience changes in their social circle, as they may lose friendships or even connections with family members who were once close due to their ties with the ex-spouse. This loss of social support can be difficult and can lead to feelings of loneliness and isolation. However, there are steps you can take to build a new support network:

- **Reach out to friends and family:** While some relationships may change after a divorce, many friends and family members may be supportive and understanding. Reach out to those who you feel comfortable talking to and let them know how they can help you.

- **Join support groups:** Consider joining a divorce support group or attending counselling sessions. This can be a helpful way to connect with others who are going through a similar experience and to gain emotional support and guidance.

- **Pursue new interests:** Joining a new club or activity can be a great way to meet new people who share your interests. This can also help you to find a sense of purpose and fulfillment outside of your previous relationship.

- **Use online resources:** So many online resources and communities can provide support during a divorce. These may include forums, blogs, and social media groups.

By reaching out to friends and family, joining support groups, pursuing new interests, and using online resources, you can find the support and connection you need to move forward.

Embrace Self-care

Taking care of yourself is crucial during this period of change. Prioritize activities that nourish both your body and mind:

Physical Well-being:

Taking care of your physical well-being is one of the best things you can do for yourself, especially during difficult times. Movement has a way of lifting your mood, relieving stress, and giving you a sense of control when everything feels overwhelming. The key is to find something you enjoy—whether it's walking, yoga, dancing, or even just stretching. It doesn't have to be intense; it just needs to make you feel good in your own body.

For me, dance, volunteering in the community, and journaling became essential parts of my self-care during my healing journey. I also spent a lot of time gardening with my children, and before we knew it, we had the most beautiful rose garden in the neighborhood. Involving them in these activities made it even more meaningful, and over time, they started journaling too. It became a shared way for us to heal, express ourselves, and bond.

I realized that movement wasn't just about staying active—it was about reconnecting with myself and creating moments of joy. Some days, I would take long walks to clear my mind; other days, I'd dance around the living room with my children to shake off heavy emotions. We even had a fun game called "Pillow Heads," where we'd balance pillows on our heads and dance around the room, laughing the entire time. Those small moments of movement helped all of us release stress, boost our energy, and remind ourselves that we were still strong.

If you're struggling, I encourage you to find an activity that brings you joy. It doesn't have to be perfect or structured—it just needs to make you feel good. You might be surprised at how much it helps, not just physically, but emotionally too.

- **Emotional Healing**: Engage in practices like meditation, journaling, or deep breathing exercises to manage stress and enhance emotional resilience.

- **Healthy Living**: Maintain a balanced diet and ensure you get adequate sleep. A healthy body supports a healthy mind.

Seek Out Support

Don't hesitate to lean on your support network during this time.

- **Family and Friends**: Surround yourself with people who uplift and encourage you. Share your feelings and experiences with them to feel understood and less alone.

- **Professional Help**: Consider therapy to work through emotional challenges and gain new coping strategies. A therapist can offer a safe space for you to explore your feelings and navigate your journey of self-discovery.

Set and Pursue New Goals

Creating a sense of direction and purpose can be invigorating.

- **Goal Setting**: Define new personal and professional goals that resonate with your current values. Whether it's learning a new skill or pursuing a career change, goals give you something to work towards and can foster a renewed sense of purpose.

- **Personal Strengths**: Focus on and build upon your existing strengths. Recognizing and developing these can enhance your confidence and self-esteem.

Redefine Your Identity

Transforming your sense of self involves exploring and embracing new aspects of who you are.

- **Discover New Interests**: Experiment with hobbies and activities that you've always wanted to try. This exploration can reveal new passions and enhance your sense of self.

- **Connect with New People**: Building new relationships can offer fresh perspectives and support. Engage in community activities or join groups aligned with your interests.

- **Adapt to Change**: Embrace the changes brought by your divorce. View them as opportunities to reinvent yourself and align with your evolving life circumstances.

Reflect and Reimagine

Take time to reflect on what truly matters to you.

- **Assess Values**: Consider what you value most in life now and how these values can guide your new goals and aspirations.

- **Explore and Evolve**: Be open to exploring new career paths, learning opportunities, and social circles. Evolution is a natural part of this journey and can lead to a more fulfilling and authentic life.

Rebuilding after a divorce is a gradual process, but with patience and persistence, you can redefine yourself in ways that bring you joy and fulfillment. Embrace the journey with openness and courage, knowing that you have the power to create a vibrant and meaningful new chapter in your life.

Set New Goals:

Setting new goals after a divorce is not just about filling the void left behind—it's a profound act of self-care and empowerment. Divorce can often leave you feeling lost, uncertain, and unsure of what's next. But by setting intentional goals, you can regain a sense of control, restore your purpose, and start building the future you truly desire. It's your opportunity to not only define what's next but to reclaim the power over your life and take an active role in creating a new chapter.

When you set goals, you affirm that your story is far from over—it's just beginning. It's an acknowledgment that, despite the challenges you've faced, you still have dreams, desires, and untapped potential to explore. Through goal setting, you turn the page and begin to focus on the future rather than what's behind you. The act of setting goals isn't about escaping the past—it's about using your experiences to fuel your growth and redefine what's possible.

Start by taking some time to reflect on your values and what truly matters to you now. Think about what lights you up, what makes you feel purposeful, and what you want to work towards. These goals can span personal, professional, and relational aspects of your life, and they should be reflective of your new identity, post-divorce.

Creating a **clear action plan** is essential to making your goals a reality. Break down each goal into smaller, actionable steps and set deadlines to hold yourself accountable. It's important to track your progress but also to remain flexible. Life after divorce is full of unexpected twists, and you might find that some goals evolve or shift as you grow. Allow yourself the grace to reassess and redefine your goals as your journey unfolds.

Setting new goals is a powerful way to reclaim your life after divorce. It's an affirmation that you are not just a victim of circumstance, but an active creator of your future. By setting meaningful goals and pursuing them with determination, you are building a life that reflects your true potential, showing yourself that you are resilient, strong, and capable of thriving in this new phase of your life. This is your time to rise, redefine yourself, and step boldly into the future you've always wanted.

Here is a comprehensive guide to setting and achieving your new goals:

1. Define Your Goals

- **Short-Term Goals**: These are objectives you want to achieve in the near future, typically within the next few months. Short-term goals often serve as stepping stones toward your long-term ambitions. Examples might include starting a new hobby, taking a course, or improving your daily routine.

- **Long-Term Goals**: These are broader objectives that you aim to accomplish over a longer period, such as a year or more. Long-term goals often require sustained effort and planning. Examples could be pursuing a new career, buying a home, or completing a degree.

2. Create SMART Goals

To ensure your goals are clear and attainable, use the SMART criteria:

- **Specific**: Clearly define what you want to achieve. Instead of "I want to get fit," say "I want to run a 5k race in three months."

- **Measurable**: Determine how you will measure your progress. For example, "I will track my running distance and time each week."

- **Achievable**: Ensure your goals are realistic given your current resources and constraints. Set challenging yet feasible objectives.

- **Relevant**: Align your goals with your broader life values and priorities. For instance, if health is a priority, focus on fitness-related goals.

- **Time-Bound**: Set a deadline for achieving your goals to stay motivated and accountable.

3. Develop an Action Plan

- **Break Down Goals**: Divide each goal into smaller, manageable tasks or milestones. For example, if your goal is to start a new career, tasks might include researching job opportunities, updating your resume, and networking.

- **Create a Timeline**: Establish a schedule for completing each task. Use a calendar or planner to allocate time for each step and track deadlines.

- **Identify Resources**: Determine what resources or support you need to achieve your goals. This could include courses, tools, or professional advice.

4. Stay Accountable

- **Track Progress**: Regularly review your progress towards your goals. Use a journal, app, or spreadsheet to monitor your achievements and adjust your plan as needed.

- **Celebrate Milestones**: Acknowledge and celebrate your successes, no matter how small. This helps maintain motivation and reinforces positive behavior.

- **Seek Support**: Share your goals with friends, family, or a mentor who can offer encouragement and hold you accountable.

5. Adjust as Needed

- **Be Flexible**: Life can be unpredictable, and your goals or circumstances might change. Be open to adjusting your goals and action plan as needed while staying focused on your overall vision.

- **Reflect and Reevaluate**: Periodically reassess your goals to ensure they still align with your evolving values and priorities. Make adjustments to keep them relevant and achievable.

6. Maintain Motivation

- **Visualize Success**: Imagine the benefits and positive outcomes of achieving your goals. Visualization can enhance motivation and clarify your commitment.

- **Stay Positive**: Keep a positive mindset and remind yourself of your progress. Focus on what you've accomplished rather than what remains to be done.

Incorporate Enjoyable Activities: Finding joy in everyday activities is a crucial part of healing and rebuilding your life. When you're going through a difficult time, it's easy to get stuck in the heaviness of emotions, but making time for things that bring you happiness—even in small ways—can make all the difference. Whether it's reading, painting, gardening, dancing, or simply enjoying a cup of coffee.

Divorce is a major life change that can leave you feeling uncertain about your future, but setting goals can give you a sense of purpose and direction. Here are some tips for setting goals after a divorce:

- **Start small:** Setting small, achievable goals can help build momentum and boost your confidence. Choose goals that are within reach and that you can accomplish in a relatively short amount of time.

- **Focus on the present:** While it's important to have long-term goals, focusing too much on the future can be overwhelming. Instead, focus on what you can do today to move closer to your goals.

- **Be specific:** Vague goals are harder to achieve than specific ones. Be clear about what you want to accomplish and set a timeline for when you want to achieve it.

- **Make your goals measurable:** Measurable goals allow you to track your progress and celebrate your successes. For example, if your goal is to get in shape, set a specific weight or fitness goal that you can track over time.

- **Consider professional help:** If you're struggling to set goals or find direction after a divorce, consider working with a therapist or life coach. They can help you identify your values, strengths, and interests, and create a plan for moving forward.

Remember, setting goals after a divorce is about creating a new vision for your life and moving forward with purpose. By starting small, focusing on the present, being specific and measurable, and seeking professional help if needed, you can create a roadmap for a brighter future.

Connect with new people: Meeting new people can help you broaden your horizons and expand your social circle. Join a new club or group or attend social events to connect with like-minded individuals.

Here are some tips for meeting new people after a divorce:

- **Join clubs or groups:** Joining a club or group that aligns with your interests can be a great way to meet new people who share your hobbies and passions. Look for local groups that focus on activities you enjoy, such as hiking, cooking, or reading.

- **Attend social events:** Attending social events such as parties, happy hours, or networking events can be a great way to meet new people. Even if you don't know anyone at the event, be open to striking up a conversation and introducing yourself.

- **Volunteer:** Volunteering for a cause that you care about can be a great way to meet like-minded people while giving back to your community. Look for local organizations that align with your values and interests.

- **Try online dating:** Online dating can be a good way to meet new people and potentially find a new romantic partner. There are many online dating sites and apps available, so do some research to find one that works for you.

- **Attend support groups:** Attending a support group for people who have gone through a divorce can be a great way to connect with others who understand what you're going through. These groups can provide emotional support and practical advice for navigating life after divorce.

Remember, meeting new people after a divorce can take time and effort. Be patient with yourself and focus on building authentic connections with others. By joining clubs or groups, attending social events, volunteering, trying online dating, and attending support groups, you can expand your social circle and create new connections that can enrich your life.

Embrace Change

Reinventing your identity requires embracing change and being open to new experiences. Don't be afraid to step outside of your comfort zone and try new things. Here are some tips for embracing change:

- **Challenge your limiting beliefs:** Identify any beliefs or assumptions that may be holding you back and challenge them. Ask yourself if these beliefs are based on facts or if they are simply self-limiting thoughts.

- **Try new things:** Step outside of your comfort zone and try new experiences. This can be as simple as trying a new hobby or as big as taking a trip to a new place.

- **Take risks:** Don't be afraid to take calculated risks in your personal or professional life. This can help you build confidence and expand your comfort zone.

- **Focus on the present**: Try to stay present in the moment and focus on what you can control right now. Avoid ruminating on the past or worrying about the future. Mindfulness practices can help with this.

Remember, change can be difficult and uncomfortable, but it can also be an opportunity for growth and self-discovery. By challenging your limiting beliefs, trying new things, taking risks, focusing on the present, and practicing mindfulness, you can embrace change and create a fulfilling life after divorce.

Practice Self-compassion

Be kind and patient with yourself as you navigate this transition. Remember that it's okay to make mistakes and that growth takes time.

Going through a divorce can be a difficult and emotional experience, and it's important to be kind and patient with yourself as you navigate this transition. Here are some tips for practicing self-compassion during this time:

- **Treat yourself with kindness:** Treat yourself with the same kindness and understanding you would offer to a close friend who's facing a tough time.

- **Acknowledge Your Emotions**: It's okay to feel a wide range of emotions during this period. Allow yourself to experience and process these feelings without judgment.

- **Prioritize Self-Care**: Attend to your physical and emotional needs by ensuring you get enough rest, eat nutritious foods, and engage in activities that make you feel happy and relaxed.

- **Practice Mindfulness**: Focus on the present moment through mindfulness techniques like meditation or deep breathing. These practices can help you manage stress and anxiety more effectively.

- **Reach Out for Support**: Don't hesitate to connect with friends, family, or a therapist who can offer emotional support and guidance during this time.

Remember that healing and growth take time, and it's important to be patient and kind to yourself during this process. Allow yourself to make mistakes, learn from them, and continue moving forward toward a happier and healthier future.

Seek Professional Help: Reinventing Your Identity with the Support of a Therapist, Life Coach, or Counselor

Reinventing your identity after a significant life change, like a divorce or personal loss, can feel overwhelming. It's easy to feel lost or unsure of where to start when trying to define who you are in this new chapter. However, you don't have to navigate this journey alone. Seeking professional help from a therapist, life coach, or counselor can be a transformative step toward rediscovering yourself, finding clarity, and building a future aligned with your values and desires.

A therapist, life coach, or counselor can be an invaluable guide in helping you redefine your identity, offering tailored support and tools to help you through the process. Here's a breakdown of how these professionals can assist you in your journey of reinvention:

- **Clarifying Your Values and Goals**: A therapist, life coach, or counselor can help you dig deep into your core values and beliefs, which are essential for creating a solid foundation for your new identity. By exploring what truly matters to you—beyond past roles and relationships—you can gain a clearer understanding of your motivations and set meaningful goals that align with your true self.

- **Processing Emotional Pain**: Reinventing yourself often involves healing from past wounds, such as the emotional scars of a divorce, betrayal, or loss. A therapist or counselor provides a safe space to process these emotions without judgment. Through techniques like talk therapy, cognitive-behavioral therapy (CBT), or mindfulness practices, they can help you navigate the emotional challenges that arise when reshaping your sense of self. Life coaches also offer valuable emotional support by helping you develop the resilience needed to move forward.

- **Building Self-Confidence**: Reinvention requires a sense of self-belief, which can be difficult to cultivate after experiencing a setback or change. A therapist, counselor, or life coach can help you challenge negative beliefs and self-doubt, replacing them with affirmations of your strengths and capabilities. With their guidance, you'll learn to develop healthier self-esteem and trust in your ability to create the life you want.

- **Developing New Coping Strategies**: Life transitions can be stressful, and these professionals can help you develop new coping mechanisms to deal with the uncertainty and emotional turbulence that often accompany reinvention. Whether it's learning relaxation techniques, mindfulness, or building resilience through reframing your challenges, a therapist, counselor, or life coach will provide you with tools to face obstacles with greater strength and adaptability.

- **Identifying Limiting Beliefs**: Often, we hold onto beliefs that hinder our growth, such as the idea that we're defined by past failures or that we're not capable of change. A therapist, counselor, or life coach can help you identify and break free from these limiting beliefs, replacing them with empowering narratives that support your reinvention and personal growth.

- **Creating an Action Plan for Change**: Reinvention is not just about shifting your mindset—it's about taking practical steps toward the future you want. A therapist, counselor, or life coach can work with you to create a personalized action plan, setting realistic, achievable goals to move you closer to your new identity. With their help, you can break down the process of reinvention into manageable steps and stay accountable as you make progress.

- **Providing Unbiased Perspective and Support**: During times of reinvention, it's easy to feel isolated or unsure of yourself. A therapist, life coach, or counselor offers an unbiased, compassionate perspective that can help you see your situation from a fresh angle. They provide emotional support without judgment, helping you stay grounded as you make the changes necessary to create a life that reflects your true desires and values.

- **Strengthening Relationships**: Reinventing your identity often involves redefining your relationships with others—whether that's family, friends, or even your ex-partner. A therapist or counselor can assist you in setting healthy boundaries, improving communication, and fostering relationships that align with your new sense of self. Life coaches can also provide guidance on how to attract and nurture positive, supportive relationships that empower you during your transformation.

- **Facilitating Long-Term Transformation**: Reinvention is a journey, not a destination. A therapist, counselor, or life coach helps you create lasting change by guiding you through the process of self-discovery and continuous personal growth. They provide the ongoing support and tools you need to sustain your transformation long after the initial phase of reinvention.

Incorporating a therapist, counselor, or life coach into your reinvention process can accelerate healing, empower you to embrace your true potential, and provide the guidance needed to make lasting changes. By seeking professional help, you are taking an essential step toward creating a future that reflects the person you are becoming—stronger, more resilient, and aligned with your authentic self. A coach or therapist can play a crucial role in helping you reinvent your identity by providing tailored support, tools, and guidance. By leveraging their expertise, you can navigate this challenging time with greater clarity and confidence, paving the way for a renewed and fulfilling sense of self.

Reinventing Your Identity After Divorce: A Journey of Self-Discovery and Empowerment

Reinventing your identity after a divorce can be one of the most challenging yet profoundly rewarding experiences of your life. It's an opportunity for growth, self-discovery, and the chance to create a life that is deeply aligned with your true self. While the process can be difficult, remember that it is not about losing who you are, but rather about shedding the roles that no longer serve you and discovering new ways to thrive on your own terms.

After spending years as part of a couple, the dissolution of that partnership often leaves you questioning who you are without the familiar role of being a wife, a partner, or even a family member within that context. The shift can feel disorienting, and at times, it may seem like you no longer exist as you once did. But this is exactly the moment to reconnect with your authentic self and redefine your identity.

So, how do you begin? It starts by taking a step back and reflecting on the person you are apart from the relationship you've left behind. Start by making a list of things you love about yourself that are independent of your former role as a spouse. What are your strengths, your talents, and the unique qualities that define you? When do you feel most empowered, happiest, or proud of who you are? What values are most important to you?

These questions may feel challenging, but they are essential to your journey of self-reinvention. By reconnecting with the aspects of yourself that are separate from the marriage, you begin to create the foundation for the next chapter of your life. You are not defined by your relationship; you are defined by the strength, resilience, and passion within you.

This process takes time, patience, and a great deal of self-compassion. Allow yourself the grace to evolve and explore new possibilities. Whether it's diving into new hobbies, expanding your career, or simply nurturing your mental and physical well-being, this is your opportunity to reshape your life in a way that honors who you are now.

Remember, reinvention is not about perfection or immediate results—it's about taking small, intentional steps toward becoming the person you were always meant to be. Through patience, self-love, and the right support, you can create a life that is even more fulfilling and meaningful than before. This is your time to thrive, embrace change, and rediscover the amazing person you are.

My Own Journey of Rediscovery and Empowerment

Reinventing my identity after my divorce was not easy. At first, I felt like I had lost myself in the process. The role I had played as a wife and partner had defined so much of who I thought I was. But I knew, deep down, that I had to find my way back to myself—outside of the marriage and everything that came with it. Here are the steps I took to reinvent myself, rebuild my life, and ultimately, find fulfillment once again.

Reconnecting with My Passions
After the divorce, I realized how much I had abandoned the things I loved. My hobbies, passions, and even career aspirations had been put on the back burner. I even give up a great job so that I could focus on my children.

But I took the time to ask myself: *What brings me joy?*

I rediscovered my love for dancing, writing, and storytelling. I had always enjoyed creating but had put it aside during my marriage. Reconnecting with my creativity helped me feel more like myself again. I also took up yoga, something I had always wanted to try but never had the time for. These activities allowed me to reconnect with my authentic self and rediscover the things that made me feel fulfilled and empowered.

Building New Relationships
One of the hardest things I faced was the change in my social circle. I had lost some friends who were connected to my ex-husband, and the community I had once been a

part of now felt unfamiliar. I had to learn to embrace the discomfort of being on my own.

I actively sought out new connections, joining social groups that aligned with my interests, like volunteering. I reached out to old friends I had lost touch with and began reconnecting with people who uplifted and supported me. It was a slow process, but with each new relationship I cultivated, I felt more grounded and connected to the world around me.

Exploring New Career Paths

The divorce had shaken not only my personal life but also my professional life. I had spent years focusing on the needs of the family, but once I was on my own, I realized I needed to build a career that reflected my own passions and aspirations.

I started exploring new career options and eventually took a leap of faith into becoming a life coach. This decision was not easy, but it was one that I felt deep down would allow me to empower others who were going through similar struggles. Building a new career from scratch gave me a renewed sense of purpose and fulfillment. It wasn't just about financial independence but about rediscovering my value outside of being a wife and mother.

Learning to Set Healthy Boundaries

A major part of redefining my identity was learning to set healthy boundaries, especially with my ex-husband. For years, I had been accustomed to putting the needs of others before my own, often at the expense of my own well-being.

I had to learn how to assert my needs, both with him and with others in my life. I practiced saying "no" when necessary and standing firm in my decisions. I also sought therapy to help me navigate difficult conversations and to work through the emotional challenges of co-parenting. Setting boundaries empowered me to take control of my own life and honor my own needs.

Embracing Self-Care

In the midst of everything, I realized that self-care was no longer optional—it was essential. For so long, I had neglected my own well-being in the service of others. But after the divorce, I understood that in order to heal and move forward, I needed to take care of myself physically, mentally, and emotionally.

I began practicing mindfulness and meditation, carving out time for rest and relaxation. I also started going for long walks in nature, something I had always enjoyed but never had time for before. These small but significant changes allowed me to reconnect with myself and heal from the emotional trauma of the divorce.

Reaffirming My Self-Worth

Finally, I had to learn to love and value myself again. Divorce had chipped away at my self-esteem, and for a long time, I doubted my worth. I had to practice self-compassion and remind myself daily that I am enough, just as I am.

I worked with a therapist who helped me challenge the negative beliefs I had about myself and build a new narrative.

I began celebrating small victories and acknowledging my strengths. I learned to embrace my imperfections and accept that I am worthy of love, respect, and happiness.

Creating a New Vision for My Future

With all the changes I made, I began to see myself not as someone defined by my past, but as someone capable of creating a future that was entirely my own. I set new goals for myself—goals that were aligned with my values and passions.

Whether it was pursuing further education, growing my coaching business, or focusing on personal growth, I took small but purposeful steps toward building a life that reflected who I am today, not who I was yesterday.

The journey of reinventing yourself after divorce is deeply personal and ongoing. It takes time, patience, and resilience, but through it all, I discovered that I am more than my past. I am capable of creating a life that aligns with my true self, and I am worthy of all the happiness and fulfillment that comes with that. If you're going through a similar journey, know that you too can reclaim your identity, embrace your strength, and build a future filled with purpose and joy.

CHAPTER THREE

Navigating the Single Life

NAVIGATING THE SINGLE LIFE

Embracing Change: A Journey of Self-Discovery and Growth

Rediscovering Yourself – Thriving in the Single Life Ahead

Navigating the single life after a divorce can feel overwhelming, but it can also be a transformative time filled with self-discovery, empowerment, and the opportunity for new beginnings. It's important to shift your perspective and embrace this chapter as a time to rediscover yourself, redefine your goals, and cultivate a fulfilling life. Here's how you can navigate the single life with confidence, strength, and purpose:

Rediscover Your True Self

Divorce provides a chance to reconnect with the person you were before your marriage, and perhaps, uncover parts of yourself you may have neglected. This is your moment to rediscover your passions, your identity, and your desires.

- **Reflect on Your Passions**: Take time to revisit hobbies, interests, and activities that once brought you joy but may have been sidelined. Whether it's painting, dancing, writing, or gardening, immerse yourself in what makes your heart sing.

- **Set Personal Goals**: Ask yourself, "What do I truly want for me now?" Whether it's mastering a new skill, starting a fitness routine, or launching a personal project, let these goals be a reflection of who you are today.

- **Explore Your Identity**: Use journaling, therapy, or simply quiet reflection to dive deep into who you are and what makes you fulfilled. This process of rediscovery can be an enlightening journey, revealing desires and strengths you may have forgotten.

Cultivate a Positive Mindset

Your mindset is a powerful tool in transforming your singlehood into an opportunity for growth. By focusing on gratitude, reframing challenges, and celebrating every step forward, you can shift from survival mode to thriving.

- **Practice Daily Gratitude**: Commit to writing down three things you are grateful for each day. This simple habit can help shift your focus from what's missing to what's abundant in your life.

- **Reframe Challenges as Opportunities**: Every challenge is a stepping stone for growth. For example, learning to manage your finances independently can be an empowering lesson in self-sufficiency and resilience.

- **Celebrate Small Wins**: Acknowledge and celebrate each milestone, no matter how small it may seem. Whether it's completing a task, trying something new, or simply spending time doing something you love, recognizing your progress builds confidence.

Expand Your Social Circle

Now is the time to surround yourself with supportive, inspiring people who uplift you. Expanding your social circle can not only bring joy but also provide fresh perspectives and new connections.

- **Engage in Shared Interests**: Whether it's joining a local book club, fitness group, or community volunteer project, these settings are natural places to meet like-minded individuals and form genuine connections.

- **Strengthen Existing Relationships**: Reach out to friends and family members you've lost touch with or spent less time with. Rekindling these relationships can provide a strong support network during this time of transition.

- **Network with Purpose**: Attend events, workshops, or gatherings with an open mind and curiosity. These encounters can lead to meaningful connections, collaborations, and even new friendships.

Embrace the Power of Solo Activities

Learning to enjoy your own company is one of the most empowering steps you can take toward self-love and independence. Being comfortable on your own means you can truly enjoy the present without relying on anyone else.

- **Take Yourself on Dates**: Plan solo outings to do things you'd normally do with a partner—visit a museum, take a hike, or enjoy a meal at your favorite restaurant. These solo experiences can build your confidence and help you reconnect with yourself.

- **Travel Alone**: Embark on a solo adventure, whether it's a weekend getaway or a trip abroad. Traveling alone allows you to set your own pace, make spontaneous decisions, and experience new things on your terms.

- **Create Rituals for Yourself**: Dedicate regular time to activities that bring you joy, like a weekly movie night, self-care routine, or quiet reading time. These personal rituals can provide comfort and a sense of peace.

Set Healthy Boundaries

Boundaries are essential for maintaining your emotional well-being and protecting your newfound independence. Being clear about your limits with others—especially your ex-spouse, family, or friends—ensures you have the space to heal and grow.

- **Define Your Limits**: Reflect on what you need to feel safe and supported, and be clear about what crosses the line. This might mean limiting contact with your ex or setting boundaries around family involvement in your personal matters.

- **Practice Assertive Communication**: Express your needs with clarity and confidence using "I" statements. For example, "I need some space right now to process my emotions" is respectful yet firm.

- **Enforce Consistency**: Once you establish boundaries, stay committed to them. It may feel uncomfortable at first, but consistency is key in maintaining your emotional health.

Prioritize Self-Care

In the midst of change, self-care becomes more than a luxury—it's a necessity for your emotional and physical well-being. Taking care of yourself allows you to build the foundation for a fulfilling single life.

- **Establish a Healthy Routine**: Build daily habits that include physical activity, nutritious meals, and quality sleep. A simple morning walk or making a smoothie can set a positive tone for the day.

- **Recharge Emotionally**: Make time for practices that help you feel grounded, such as journaling, mindfulness, or spending time with uplifting friends and family.

- **Celebrate Your Progress**: Recognize the importance of prioritizing yourself. Every step you take toward self-care is a victory.

Embrace New Experiences

Stepping out of your comfort zone and trying new things can completely transform your perspective and expand your horizons. Embrace the unknown with curiosity and excitement.

- **Start Small**: If trying new things feels daunting, start with simple experiences—like trying a new recipe or visiting a different café. Small steps build confidence.

- **Explore Your Community**: Attend local workshops, art exhibits, or community festivals. These experiences can introduce you to new people, perspectives, and passions.

- **Document Your Journey**: Keep a journal or photo diary of your adventures and reflect on your growth along the way. Celebrating new experiences will help you stay motivated.

Build a Strong Support System

Having a supportive network can make all the difference during this transition. Surround yourself with people who believe in you and lift you up.

- **Reconnect with Loved Ones**: Reach out to family and friends you may have lost touch with. Rebuilding these connections can offer a sense of comfort and belonging.

- **Find Your Tribe**: Seek out groups or communities that align with your interests and values. Whether it's an online forum, a fitness group, or a spiritual circle, being around people who share your passions is empowering.

- **Seek Professional Help**: A therapist, counselor, or life coach can provide invaluable support and guidance during this transition, helping you navigate your emotions and gain perspective.

Invest in Yourself

Your personal growth is the best investment you can make. By focusing on your own happiness and fulfillment, you build a foundation for a future full of possibility.

- **Learn Something New**: Take a class or workshop in a subject that interests you—whether it's something creative, professional, or purely for fun.

- **Travel**: Take the opportunity to travel, whether to a nearby city or an international destination. New experiences can broaden your perspective and enrich your life.

- **Volunteer**: Find a cause you're passionate about and dedicate your time to helping others. Volunteering can provide a sense of purpose and connection.

Find New Hobbies and Interests

Rediscovering old passions or trying new ones can be a fulfilling way to spend your time and energy.

- **Try New Activities**: Sign up for classes or workshops in areas that interest you—painting, dancing, cooking, or photography, for example. Experiment with no pressure to master them, just to enjoy the process.

- **Balance Fun and Growth**: Pursue hobbies that are both fun and enriching. Learning a new language or cooking healthy meals can be both enjoyable and personally beneficial.

- **Stay Open-Minded**: Let your interests evolve as you grow. Hobbies don't have to be permanent—they can change as you discover more about yourself.

Embrace New Opportunities

Being single is not an end—it's a beginning. It's a chance to create the life you want on your own terms, free from the constraints of the past.

- **Say "Yes" to New Experiences**: Don't be afraid to step outside your comfort zone. Accept invitations to social events or try something spontaneous.

- **Approach Opportunities with Curiosity**: Embrace the unknown with a "Why not?" mindset. You never know what might come from saying yes to new experiences.

Focus on Personal Growth

The most valuable investment you can make is in yourself. Focus on growth, learning, and self-improvement, and watch how it transforms your life.

- **Set Meaningful Goals**: Whether it's personal development, career growth, or emotional resilience, set goals that push you to become your best self.

- **Create a Self-Improvement Plan**: Read books, listen to podcasts, or take courses that inspire you. The key is to continuously invest in your growth.

- **Track Your Progress**: Regularly reflect on how far you've come. Journaling or self-assessments can provide a sense of accomplishment and motivation.

By incorporating these strategies into your single life, you're setting the stage for personal growth, independence, and fulfillment. Remember, being single isn't a limitation—it's an opportunity to reinvent yourself and create a life that reflects your true desires and aspirations. Embrace this time as a journey of empowerment, self-love, and limitless possibilities.

CHAPTER FOUR

Navigating Child Custody

Navigating child custody arrangements is often one of the most emotionally and logistically challenging aspects of divorce. It requires careful consideration, open communication, and a shared commitment to the well-being of the child or children involved.

Whether you're establishing initial custody agreements or modifying existing arrangements, approaching the process with sensitivity and respect for each other's roles as parents is crucial.

Effective communication is fundamental. Clear, honest discussions about schedules, responsibilities, and decision-making can help prevent misunderstandings and reduce conflicts. It's important to listen actively to each other's concerns and priorities, aiming for compromises that prioritize the child's stability and happiness.

Flexibility is another vital aspect. Life circumstances can change unexpectedly, requiring adjustments to custody arrangements. Being open to discussing and renegotiating terms when necessary demonstrates a willingness to adapt for the child's best interests.

Seeking professional guidance may also be beneficial. Family counselors, mediators, or lawyers specializing in family law can provide objective advice and help facilitate constructive discussions. They can also offer insights into legal rights and responsibilities, ensuring that decisions align with both legal requirements and the child's needs.

Above all, maintaining a child-centered approach is key. Children thrive when they feel secure in their relationships with both parents. Encouraging positive interactions and shared experiences, even after divorce, can foster a stable environment where the child feels supported and loved by both parents.

Navigating child custody together requires patience, empathy, and a commitment to cooperation. By focusing on effective communication, flexibility, professional guidance when needed, and keeping the child's well-being at the forefront, parents can navigate this challenging process in a way that supports the child's healthy development and overall happiness.

Navigating child custody arrangements during a divorce can feel overwhelming, but understanding the legal framework is essential for ensuring the best interests of your child are prioritized. This knowledge not only supports a smoother transition but also fosters stability for both you and your child during this challenging time. Here's a breakdown of key considerations when it comes to child custody:

1. Types of Child Custody:

Child custody can take on different forms, each with distinct implications for both parents and children:

- **Sole Custody:** One parent takes primary responsibility for the child's care and decision-making. The other parent typically has visitation or access rights, though they are not involved in major decisions.

- **Joint Custody:** Both parents share the responsibility for decision-making in their child's life. While one parent may have the child living with them most of the time, both remain deeply involved in important decisions.

- **Shared Custody:** Children split their time between both parents, ensuring meaningful and frequent contact with both. This arrangement works best when parents are capable of maintaining cooperation and communication.

2. Legal Framework and Laws:

Child custody laws around the world center around one thing: what is in the **best interests of the child**. Courts carefully consider a number of factors, including the child's preference if possible, when determining custody arrangements and understanding these can help parents make informed decisions.

3. Parenting Plans and Agreements:

A solid parenting plan or agreement can help avoid future conflicts and ensure both parents are on the same page.

- **Components of a Parenting Plan:** A good plan includes custody arrangements (sole, joint, or shared), visitation schedules, and decision-making powers about areas like healthcare, education, and major life choices.

- **Mediation and Negotiation:** Rather than going to court, parents are often encouraged to resolve their disagreements through mediation. A neutral third-party mediator can help facilitate discussions and find a compromise that respects everyone's needs.

- **Legal Assistance:** When drafting a parenting plan, it's beneficial to consult a family lawyer to ensure the agreement is legally sound and protects parental rights. They can also help ensure the plan reflects the best interests of the child.

4. Enforcement and Modifications:

Understanding how custody orders are enforced and when they can be modified is crucial.

- **Enforcement:** If one parent fails to follow a custody agreement—such as denying the other parent access to their child—legal remedies can be pursued, including court orders to ensure compliance.

- **Modifications:** Life circumstances change, and so can custody arrangements. If one parent relocates or there is a significant shift in parental ability to care for the child, custody arrangements may be modified. The court will evaluate any proposed changes based on what is in the child's best interests.

5. Additional Considerations:

There are several other factors that may come into play during the custody process:

- **Relocation:** If one parent intends to move with the child, the other parent must be notified, and in some cases, the move may need to be approved by the court.

- **Grandparents' Rights:** In some situations, grandparents may seek visitation rights if they had a significant relationship with the child. The court will consider the child's well-being when making these decisions.

- **International Issues:** If a parent intends to move abroad with the child, it can complicate custody arrangements. Legal advice becomes critical to navigate cross-border issues and international custody treaties.

Moving Forward:

Understanding the intricacies of child custody is key to navigating a divorce with your child's best interests at heart.

By utilizing mediation, staying informed, and seeking legal counsel when needed, parents can ensure that their custody arrangement provides a stable and supportive environment for their child.

Essential Resources for Child Custody Support:

Navigating child custody can feel overwhelming, especially during a time of emotional and personal upheaval. However, you don't have to go through it alone. Numerous resources are available to help guide you through the process, ensuring that you make informed decisions in the best interest of your child. Here's a more detailed look at some of the most impactful resources that can offer crucial support:

Government Family Law Resources:
Many governments offer detailed, accessible information about family law, including custody, child support, and visitation rights. These resources are designed to help you understand your legal rights and responsibilities as a parent, as well as the steps involved in filing for custody or support. Depending on where you live, government websites may also include helpful guides, FAQs, and links to other essential resources.

Legal Aid Services:
If you're unable to afford a private lawyer, legal aid services can be a lifeline. Many regions offer free or low-cost legal assistance to those who qualify. Legal aid professionals can provide guidance on filing custody petitions, understanding

your legal options, and representing you in court if necessary.

Court Forms and Instructions:
Many courts provide free access to forms needed for filing custody-related matters. These forms may include petitions for custody, visitation requests, or modifications to existing arrangements. In addition to forms, courts often offer detailed instructions on how to complete them properly.

Community Legal Education:
Community organizations often provide free legal resources, workshops, and seminars to help individuals navigate family law issues. These resources are often written in plain language to ensure they are accessible to everyone, regardless of their legal knowledge. Some organizations may even offer legal counseling or help you understand the implications of your custody case.

Family Law Information Centres:
Many courthouses have dedicated Family Law Information Centres (FLICs) that offer support and resources related to child custody and family law matters. These centres can help guide you through the court process, provide you with court forms, and even explain the legal steps in your custody case.

Mediation and Parenting Coordination Services:
Mediation is a popular alternative to a lengthy and contentious courtroom battle. Many regions provide access to mediation services where parents can work with a neutral third party to resolve custody disputes in a less adversarial

environment. Parenting coordinators can also help parents implement and enforce custody orders post-divorce or separation.

Creating a Custody Arrangement That Works for Your Family

With the right knowledge, support, and resources, you can approach the child custody process with confidence. By educating yourself on the legal framework, exploring options like mediation, and utilizing community and professional support, you can create a custody arrangement that prioritizes your child's emotional, physical, and psychological well-being. It's not an easy road, but with the proper guidance and resources, you can navigate it in a way that fosters a healthy, stable environment for your child's future.

CHAPTER FIVE

Dating After Divorce

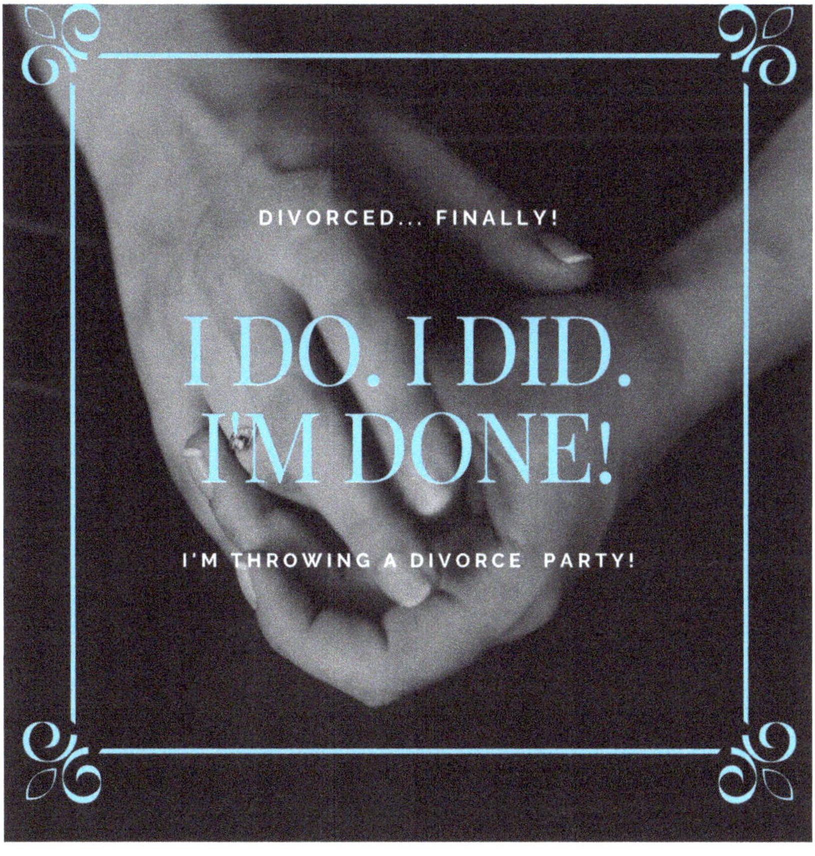

DIVORCED... FINALLY!

I DO. I DID. I'M DONE!

I'M THROWING A DIVORCE PARTY!

If you're ready to start dating again, congratulations! Dating after divorce can be exciting and daunting at the same time. Here are some tips for navigating the dating world after a divorce:

- **Give yourself time:** It's important to take the time to heal and process your emotions before jumping into a new relationship. Make sure you're emotionally ready to start dating again.

- **Be clear about your intentions:** Be honest with yourself and your potential partners about what you're looking for in a relationship.

- **Take it slow:** Don't rush into anything too quickly. Take the time to get to know someone before committing to a relationship.

- **Be open-minded:** Try not to compare new partners to your ex-spouse or hold them to the same expectations. Be open to new experiences and new types of people.

- **Communicate openly:** Be open and honest with your new partner about your past and your feelings. Communication is key to any successful relationship.

- **Set healthy boundaries:** It's important to establish boundaries and communicate your needs and expectations in a new relationship.

- **Don't involve your children too soon:** If you have children, take your time introducing them to your new partner. Make sure you're confident in the relationship before involving your children.

- **Take care of yourself:** Make sure you're taking care of yourself physically and emotionally as you navigate the dating world. Don't neglect your own needs and self-care routine.

Take time for yourself

Before jumping into a new relationship, take time to focus on yourself and heal from your divorce. Taking time to heal and focus on yourself is important before entering a new relationship after a divorce. This allows for self-discovery, personal growth, and reflection on what one wants and needs in a partner. It's essential to process and deal with the emotions from the previous relationship to avoid bringing any baggage or unresolved issues into a new relationship.

It's also important to set realistic expectations for dating after divorce. Don't rush into anything, and take the time to get to know someone before committing to a serious relationship. It's essential to communicate your needs, expectations, and boundaries with a potential partner. Remember that dating after divorce is a process, and it's okay to take things at your own pace. With time, patience, and an open mind, you can find a fulfilling and healthy relationship after divorce.

Here's some advice to help you build confidence, navigate the dating world, and avoid common pitfalls:

Focus on building your confidence: Confidence is key when it comes to dating. Having confidence in yourself is an important aspect of dating after divorce. Remember that you are worthy of love and to approach dating with a positive attitude. Focus on your strengths and what makes you unique, and try to let go of any negative self-talk or self-doubt. Remember that confidence is attractive and can help you find healthy and fulfilling relationships. Take the time to focus on your own self-improvement, whether that means hitting the gym, taking up a new hobby, or investing in self-care. By building your confidence, you'll be more comfortable and at ease when meeting new people.

Be open-minded: When it comes to dating, it's important to be open-minded and willing to try new things. This may include going on dates with people who don't fit your "type" or trying new activities or hobbies that you wouldn't normally do.

Take things slow: Taking things slow can be helpful when entering a new relationship after divorce. It allows you to fully process your emotions and get to know the person you're dating without any added pressure. Rushing into a new relationship too quickly can lead to repeating past patterns and mistakes. It's important to establish a strong foundation of friendship and trust before taking any major steps forward. This means getting to know someone before jumping into a serious relationship and taking time to assess whether you're truly compatible with them.

Be honest and authentic: Honesty and authenticity are key when it comes to dating. This means being open about your past and any potential challenges or issues that may come up in a new relationship. It's important to be true to yourself and your values and not to try to be someone you're not just to impress someone else. This can help build a foundation of trust and respect in a new relationship. Additionally, it's important to be clear about what you're looking for in a new partner and to communicate your needs and expectations clearly and honestly. Be honest about your interests, values, and intentions, and don't be afraid to be yourself. This can help you find someone who is a good match for you and who shares your goals and values. Trying to be someone you're not or pretending to be interested in things that you're not will only lead to disappointment and frustration for both you and your potential partner in the long run. You want to attract people who are genuinely interested in getting to know the real you.

Stay safe: When dating, it's essential to prioritize your safety and protect yourself. Here are some tips to help:

- **Get to know the person:** Take the time to get to know the person you are dating before agreeing to meet in person. Talk to them on the phone or video chat, and do some research to ensure they are who they say they are.

- **Meet in public places:** When you're ready to meet in person, choose a public place for your first few dates, such as a coffee shop, restaurant, or park. Avoid private or isolated places until you feel comfortable and know the person better.

- **Tell someone where you're going:** Before meeting your date, let a friend or family member know where you're going, who you're meeting, and when you plan to return. Consider sharing your date's contact information and a photo, too.

- **Trust your instincts:** If something feels off or uncomfortable during your date, trust your instincts and leave. You don't owe anyone an explanation.

- **Practice safe sex:** Protect yourself from sexually transmitted infections by using condoms and other safe sex practices.

Remember, your safety is the most important thing, so don't hesitate to take steps to protect yourself.

Avoid common pitfalls: There are many common pitfalls when it comes to dating, such as getting too attached too quickly, ignoring red flags, or settling for someone who isn't right for you. Be aware of these pitfalls and take steps to avoid them, such as setting clear boundaries and listening to your gut instincts.

Remember that dating is a journey, and it may take some time to find the right person for you. By focusing on building your confidence, being open-minded, taking things slow, being honest and authentic, staying safe, and avoiding common pitfalls, you can navigate the dating world with greater ease and success. Good luck!

CHAPTER SIX

Financial Independence

Financial independence is crucial after a divorce, as it allows you to build a stable and secure future for yourself. Divorce can often have a significant impact on a person's financial situation, and it may take time to recover. It's important to take steps to regain financial independence by creating a budget, reducing expenses, and increasing income through education, training, or seeking better job opportunities. It can also be helpful to seek out financial advice or support to help navigate the financial implications of a divorce and create a plan for moving forward. This can help individuals regain control of their finances and reduce the stress and anxiety that may come with financial instability.

Here are some tips for achieving financial independence during and after a divorce.

Create a Budget

Creating a detailed budget that takes into account your income, expenses, and debts is an important step in gaining financial stability after a divorce. Here are some steps to help you create a budget:

- **Determine your income:** This includes any money you receive from your job, child support, spousal support, or any other source.

- **List your expenses:** Make a list of all your monthly expenses, including housing, utilities, food, transportation, insurance, and any other expenses you have.

- **Categorize your expenses:** Group your expenses into categories such as housing, food, transportation, and entertainment.

- **Prioritize your expenses:** Identify which expenses are essential and which are discretionary. Prioritize your essential expenses and look for ways to reduce your discretionary spending.

- **Track your spending:** Keep track of all your expenses for at least a month. This will help you identify areas where you can cut back on spending.

- **Make adjustments:** Based on your tracking, adjust your budget to ensure you are living within your means.

- **Create a plan to pay off debt:** If you have debt, create a plan to pay it off as quickly as possible. Consider consolidating your debt or seeking the help of a financial advisor.

- **Build an emergency fund:** Set aside some money each month to build an emergency fund. This will help you handle unexpected expenses without having to rely on credit.

- **Review your budget regularly:** Review your budget regularly to ensure you are staying on track and making progress towards your financial goals.

Remember, creating a budget takes time and effort, but it can be a valuable tool in helping you gain control of your finances after a divorce.

Understand Your Assets and Debts

Understand your financial situation, including your assets and debts. This can help you negotiate a fair settlement during the divorce process and make informed financial decisions in the future. Understanding your financial situation is an important first step in creating a solid financial plan. Here are some steps to help you understand your financial situation:

1. **Gather all of your financial documents:** This includes bank statements, credit card statements, loan statements, investment account statements, tax returns, and any other financial documents you have.

   Calculate your net worth: This is the value of all your assets minus your debts. List out all your assets, including your home, car, investments, savings, and any other valuable items you own. Then, list out all your debts, including your mortgage, car loan, student loans, credit card debt, and any other debts you owe. Subtract your debts from your assets to get your net worth.

   Understanding your net worth gives you a clear picture of your financial situation, which is crucial during life transitions like divorce. It helps you see exactly where you stand financially, allowing you to make informed decisions about your future.

By calculating your net worth, you'll be able to:

- ✅ Assess Your Financial Health – Knowing how much you own versus how much you owe helps you determine whether you're in a stable financial position or need to make adjustments.

- ✅ Prepare for Negotiations – If you're going through a divorce, having a clear understanding of your assets and debts can help ensure fair division of property and prevent financial surprises.

- ✅ Plan for Your Future – Once you know your net worth, you can set realistic financial goals, whether it's saving for a new home, adjusting your budget, or planning for long-term stability.

- ✅ Avoid Overspending & Debt – When you see your full financial picture, it becomes easier to identify areas where you need to cut back or focus on paying down debt.

For me, calculating my net worth was an eye-opener. It showed me where I needed to take control of my finances and what I needed to prioritize moving forward. It gave me the confidence to make better financial decisions and build a secure foundation for myself and my children.

If you haven't done this before, take some time to write everything down—it may seem overwhelming at first, but knowledge is power. Once you have a clear understanding of your net worth, you'll feel more in control of your financial future and better prepared to take the next steps.

2. **Analyze your spending**: Look through your bank and credit card statements to see where you are spending your money. Categorize your expenses into necessary expenses (like housing, food, and utilities) and discretionary expenses (like dining out and entertainment).

3. **Review your credit report:** Your credit report is a reflection of your financial history. Make sure to check your credit report for accuracy and any potential issues that could affect your credit score.

Knowing your net worth is incredibly important when navigating a divorce. Your **net worth** is essentially the value of everything you own (your assets) minus everything you owe (your debts). Understanding this number can provide clarity and help you make informed decisions about property division, support, and long-term financial planning.

Here's why knowing your net worth is helpful during a divorce:

Fair Property Division:
Dividing assets and debts fairly is one of the most challenging aspects of a divorce. Your net worth will give both you and

your lawyer a clear understanding of your financial standing. By knowing what you own and owe, you can more easily evaluate what assets might be divided or sold, and what each spouse will receive. A balanced approach to property division starts with a complete understanding of your financial situation.

Setting Realistic Expectations:
Divorce can lead to significant changes in your lifestyle. Having a clear picture of your net worth helps set realistic expectations for both parties about how finances will look post-divorce. This understanding can help reduce conflicts, especially when it comes to deciding on spousal support or child support, since both parties will have a better sense of what's possible within their new financial realities.

Debt Allocation:
Just as assets are divided, debts are also part of the divorce settlement. Knowing your total debts—whether credit cards, loans, or mortgages—helps determine how they will be shared or assigned to either spouse. Your net worth gives a snapshot of the debts that need to be managed and allocated, ensuring that both parties have a clear understanding of financial obligations.

Financial Independence:
During divorce, it's easy to lose sight of your long-term financial independence. Knowing your net worth helps you plan for life after divorce by providing a clearer picture of what you can afford moving forward. You'll be better equipped to create a budget, manage your financial goals,

and understand your ability to maintain or change your current living arrangements, lifestyle, or retirement plans.

Negotiation Leverage:

In divorce negotiations, having an accurate net worth statement gives you the leverage you need. Whether it's negotiating property division, alimony, or child support, knowing the value of your assets and debts will provide a clear basis for your proposals. It's difficult to argue for a fair settlement without knowing what your financial picture looks like.

How to Calculate Your Net Worth:

To calculate your net worth, start by **listing all of your assets**—everything of value you own, such as:

- Bank accounts
- Retirement savings
- Investments
- Real estate
- Vehicles
- Personal property (jewelry, art, etc.)

Next, **subtract your liabilities**, or debts, including:

- Mortgages
- Credit card debt
- Personal loans
- Car loans
- Any other outstanding financial obligations

The difference between your assets and debts is your **net worth**.

Develop a Plan for Your Future

Develop a plan for your financial future, including your goals and how you plan to achieve them. Consider your short-term and long-term financial goals, such as paying off debt, saving for retirement, and building an emergency fund. Developing a plan for your financial future can help you achieve your goals and build a stable and secure future after divorce. Here are some steps to consider:

- **Set financial goals:** Determine what you want to achieve financially in the short-term and long-term. This could include paying off debt, saving for a down payment on a house, or planning for retirement.

- **Assess your income:** Determine your sources of income, including your salary, investments, and any government benefits or support payments.

- **Assess your expenses:** Track your expenses over a period of time to get a clear understanding of your spending habits. This will help you identify areas where you can cut back and save money.

- **Create a budget:** Use the information you've gathered to create a detailed budget that takes into account your income, expenses, and debts. Make sure your budget is realistic and allows you to meet your financial goals.

- **Manage your debt:** Create a plan for paying off any debts you have, starting with those that have the highest interest rates. Consider seeking professional help if you're struggling to manage your debt.

- **Save for the future:** Set aside money each month for savings and investments. Consider working with a financial planner to help you create an investment strategy that aligns with your financial goals.

- **Review and adjust your plan regularly:** Your financial situation may change over time, so it's important to review and adjust your plan regularly to ensure it still aligns with your goals and needs.

Build an Emergency Fund

Building an emergency fund can provide a financial safety net during times of financial hardship. Aim to save at least three to six months of living expenses in an emergency fund.

Here are some steps you can take to start building your emergency fund:

- **Set a goal:** Determine how much you want to save for your emergency fund. A good rule of thumb is to aim for three to six months' living expenses.

- **Create a budget:** Review your income and expenses to see where you can make adjustments to free up some money to save. Consider cutting back on non-essential expenses or finding ways to increase your income.

- **Start saving:** Once you have determined how much you want to save, start putting money aside regularly. You can set up automatic transfers from your checking account to a savings account to make it easier to save consistently.

- **Keep your emergency fund separate:** Keep your emergency fund separate from your other savings accounts and avoid using it for non-emergency expenses.

- **Re-evaluate regularly:** Review your emergency fund regularly to make sure you are on track to meet your goals. Adjust your savings plan as needed based on changes in your financial situation.

Focus on Your Career

Focusing on your career can help you increase your income and achieve financial independence. Consider pursuing additional education or training to enhance your skills and make yourself more marketable in your field.

Focusing on your career during a divorce can be a great way to take your mind off of the emotional stresses of the situation and set yourself up for a stable future. Here are some tips for focusing on your career during a divorce:

- **Set career goals:** Take some time to identify what you want to achieve in your career. Set achievable goals that can help you move forward and make progress.

- **Improve your skills:** Consider taking classes or workshops to develop new skills that can help you advance in your career.

- **Network:** Connect with other professionals in your field by attending networking events or joining industry groups. Building relationships can help you learn about new opportunities and stay up to date on industry trends.

- **Seek mentorship:** Look for mentors who can offer guidance and advice as you navigate your career. A mentor can help you set goals, overcome challenges, and make progress.

- **Keep your focus:** Remember that your career is important, but don't let it distract you from other aspects of your life. Set boundaries to maintain a healthy work-life balance.

- **Take care of yourself:** Self-care is important during a divorce, and it can help you stay focused and productive at work. Make sure to take breaks, exercise, and prioritize your mental health.

Stay Organized

Keep your financial documents organized, including tax returns, bank statements, and investment statements. This can help you stay on top of your finances and make informed financial decisions.

Remember that achieving financial independence during and after divorce is a process, and it's okay to take it one step at a time. With patience, diligence, and a focus on your financial goals, you can achieve financial independence and build a stable and secure future.

Seek Professional Advice

Seeking professional advice is one of the most important steps you can take when navigating the financial complexities of divorce. Divorce is not just an emotional process; it's also a significant financial event that can affect your long-term financial stability. A financial planner, accountant, or other financial experts can provide invaluable guidance to help you understand your options, plan for your future, and avoid costly mistakes. Here's why seeking professional advice is essential and how experts can assist you throughout the divorce process:

Comprehensive Financial Assessment

A financial planner or accountant can help you gain a full understanding of your financial situation by analyzing your assets, liabilities, income, and expenses. They can help you create a detailed financial picture that takes into account everything from retirement savings to tax liabilities, so you're fully aware of what you're dealing with. This comprehensive assessment is crucial for making informed decisions about property division, alimony, child support, and other financial matters.

Understanding Complex Financial Assets

Divorce often involves more than just basic assets like bank accounts or personal property. Many people own complex financial assets such as retirement accounts (401(k), pensions), investment portfolios, or business interests. These assets require careful evaluation to determine their true value and how they should be divided. A financial planner can help you understand how these assets are valued, how to protect them during the divorce process, and what steps are needed to divide them fairly.

For example, retirement accounts may have penalties or tax implications when divided. A financial planner or tax advisor can help you navigate these issues, ensuring that you don't end up with unexpected financial consequences later on.

Tax Implications

Divorce can have significant tax implications, especially when it comes to asset division, spousal support, and child support. For example, alimony payments are typically tax-deductible for the paying spouse, but taxable for the receiving spouse (in jurisdictions where this rule applies). Understanding how these payments will affect your tax situation is crucial for making sound financial decisions. Additionally, the division of assets such as retirement accounts, real estate, or investments may trigger capital gains taxes or penalties, depending on the nature of the assets.

An accountant or tax professional can help you understand these tax implications and advise you on the most tax-efficient way to divide assets and plan for your financial future post-divorce.

Creating a Realistic Budget Post-Divorce

One of the biggest adjustments after divorce is living on a single income. Many people are shocked by how their financial situation changes after divorce, particularly if one spouse has been the primary breadwinner. A financial advisor can help you create a realistic post-divorce budget, factoring in your new income, child support or alimony payments, and any new financial responsibilities (e.g., maintaining two households).

A financial planner can also help you identify areas where you may need to make cuts or adjustments, such as selling assets, downsizing, or finding ways to reduce expenses. This will give you a clearer idea of how to manage your money and avoid financial strain.

Planning for the Future

Divorce can leave you feeling uncertain about your future. A financial planner can help you look ahead and create a plan for your long-term financial goals, including retirement planning, savings, investments, and other key financial decisions. They can help you determine how much you should be saving, what kind of investments might be appropriate for your new financial situation, and how to ensure that your financial future remains stable.

A professional can also help you identify any gaps in your financial plan that may have been overlooked, such as emergency funds, health insurance, or college savings for children. By proactively planning for your future, you'll be better equipped to face any financial challenges ahead.

Minimizing Financial Conflict
Divorce can sometimes lead to contentious financial battles, especially if there is disagreement over asset division or alimony. Having a financial planner or accountant on your side can provide an objective, third-party perspective that helps prevent conflict. These professionals can also assist in preparing financial statements or reports that can be used in court, helping to present your financial position clearly and accurately.

Additionally, a financial planner can act as a mediator of sorts, offering solutions that might not have been considered by both parties, such as using certain assets to offset spousal support payments or proposing a creative division of retirement accounts to avoid penalties. Their guidance can help reduce tension and facilitate a more amicable resolution.

Debt Management
In many divorces, there is a shared responsibility for debts—mortgages, car loans, credit cards, and other outstanding

liabilities. A financial planner or accountant can help you create a strategy for managing and distributing these debts fairly. They can also provide advice on how to protect your credit and rebuild it post-divorce, as well as how to avoid taking on more debt than you can manage.

Child and Spousal Support Calculations

The financial aspects of child support and spousal support can be complex, especially when determining the amount, duration, and method of payment. A financial planner can help ensure that the support calculations are based on accurate financial information and that the amounts requested are fair and feasible for both parties. They can also advise you on how to adjust your financial plans if support payments change over time.

Navigating Business Interests

If you or your spouse owns a business, divorce can complicate things further. A financial advisor with expertise in business valuation can help determine the worth of the business and how it should be divided or sold. They can also help ensure that business interests are protected, and that you're not left with an unfair share of the business's debts or liabilities.

Assisting with Legal Coordination

A financial planner or accountant often works closely with divorce attorneys to ensure that all aspects of the financial settlement are handled correctly. They can help coordinate the financial elements of the divorce agreement, such as property division, asset allocation, and tax considerations, with the legal aspects of the case. This coordination can streamline the divorce process and ensure that nothing is overlooked or mishandled.

Conclusion:

Divorce is a major life event that affects not just your emotions but your finances as well. Seeking professional advice from a financial planner, accountant, or tax expert can help you navigate these complexities with more confidence and clarity. They can provide expert guidance on everything from budgeting and debt management to asset division and long-term financial planning, ensuring that you make decisions that are in your best interest. By enlisting professional support, you can avoid costly mistakes, minimize stress, and secure a solid financial foundation for your future.

CHAPTER SEVEN

Dealing with Loneliness

A Few Ways to Overcome Loneliness

Interact with strangers.

Reinforce existing relationships.

Implement self-care and self-love.

Use your money to experience new things.

It's common to experience feelings of loneliness after a divorce, as you may have lost a significant source of companionship and support. Here are some tips that may help:

Connect with others: Reach out to friends, family members, or support groups to connect with others who are going through a similar experience. You could also consider joining social clubs or volunteer organizations to meet new people.

Stay connected with friends and family: Reach out to friends and family for support and companionship. Don't hesitate to ask for help or to lean on those who care about you.

Join a support group: Consider joining a support group for people going through a divorce or for individuals who are dealing with loneliness. This can provide a safe space to share your experiences and connect with others who are going through similar struggles.

Pursue your passions: Focus on your hobbies and interests. Pursuing your passions can help you feel more fulfilled and connected to your sense of self. Engaging in activities or hobbies that bring you joy and fulfillment can help combat loneliness and provide a sense of purpose. It can also be an opportunity to meet new people who share similar interests and expand your social circle.

Volunteer: Volunteering can provide a sense of purpose and help you connect with others who share your values and interests. Volunteering can be a fulfilling way to connect with others and give back to your community. It can also provide opportunities to learn new skills and gain valuable experience. Plus, it can help you feel a sense of purpose and accomplishment, which can boost your overall mood and well-being. Whether it's volunteering at a local charity, animal shelter, or community center, there are many opportunities to get involved and make a positive impact.

Try new things: Be open to trying new things and meeting new people. This can help you build new connections and explore new opportunities for growth and happiness.

Seek professional help: Consider seeking the help of a therapist or counselor who can provide support and guidance as you navigate the challenges of divorce and loneliness.

There are many resources available to provide guidance and support during and after a divorce. Here are a few options:

- **Therapists or counsellors:** A mental health professional can provide a safe and supportive space to process your emotions and work through any challenges you may be facing.

- **Support groups:** Joining a support group for individuals who are going through or have gone through a divorce can be a helpful way to connect with others who can relate to your experiences.

- **Divorce coaches:** A divorce coach can provide guidance and support throughout the divorce process, including helping you navigate legal issues, co-parenting, and emotional challenges.

- **Online communities:** There are many online communities and forums where individuals going through a divorce can connect and share their experiences.

- **Friends and family:** Don't be afraid to reach out to trusted friends and family members for support and guidance during this challenging time.

Seeking support is a sign of strength, not weakness. There is no shame in asking for help, and taking care of your emotional and mental well-being is essential to moving forward and finding happiness after divorce.

Dealing with loneliness after a divorce is a journey that unfolds over time, and it's completely normal to approach it one step at a time. The process of overcoming loneliness is not about making swift changes but rather about gently navigating through the emotions and challenges that come with this transition. It's important to understand that healing and finding new sources of fulfillment will not happen overnight, and that's perfectly okay. Allowing yourself the space and time to feel, reflect, and grow is a vital part of this process.

Patience is your ally during this period. Rebuilding your life after a divorce involves making small, meaningful steps toward creating a new and fulfilling reality. This might include reconnecting with old friends, exploring new hobbies, or even just setting aside time for self-care. Each step, no matter how small, is a significant part of moving forward. Embrace this gradual process with an open heart, knowing that each effort you make is a step toward a more connected and satisfying life.

Self-compassion is crucial as you navigate through loneliness. Be kind to yourself as you experience the ups and downs of this transition. Understand that it's natural to have moments of doubt or sadness, and it's important to treat yourself with the same kindness and understanding you would offer a dear friend in a similar situation. Celebrate the little victories, such as engaging in a new activity or making a new connection, and recognize that these efforts are building blocks toward a richer, more fulfilling life.

Focusing on building a fulfilling life involves more than just addressing loneliness; it's about creating a new sense of purpose and joy. This might involve exploring interests you've always been passionate about, setting new personal goals, or seeking out new social connections. The key is to approach this journey with a sense of curiosity and openness, allowing yourself to discover new aspects of who you are and what brings you happiness.

In the end, the path to overcoming loneliness is deeply personal and unique to each individual. By practicing patience, embracing self-compassion, and taking gradual steps toward building a fulfilling life, you'll find that loneliness begins to ease, and a new chapter filled with potential and joy starts to unfold. Remember, you are not alone in this journey, and with time, support, and self-kindness, happiness is not only possible but within reach.

Ultimately, healing from loneliness is not about rushing the process but about allowing yourself the space to grow and rediscover joy at your own pace. It's important to acknowledge that every journey is different, and what works for one person may not work for another. However, by practicing patience, embracing self-compassion, and taking gradual steps toward building a fulfilling life, you'll find that loneliness begins to ease. As you open yourself up to new experiences and connections, a new chapter filled with potential and joy starts to unfold. Remember, you are not alone in this journey, and with time, support, and self-kindness, happiness is not only possible but within reach.

1. Engage in Creative Expression

- **Start a Creative Project**: Dive into creative activities such as painting, writing, or crafting. Creative expression can be a therapeutic way to process emotions and find joy.

- **Join an Art Class**: Enroll in an art or writing class to explore new talents and meet people with similar creative interests.

2. Adopt a Pet

- **Consider Pet Ownership**: If it fits your lifestyle, adopting a pet can provide companionship and emotional support. Animals can offer unconditional love and help alleviate feelings of loneliness.

- **Volunteer at an Animal Shelter**: If adopting a pet isn't feasible, volunteering at a shelter can give you a sense of purpose and connect you with animal lovers.

3. Explore Nature and Outdoor Activities

- **Take Nature Walks**: Spend time in nature by hiking, walking, or gardening. Being outdoors can improve your mood and provide a sense of tranquility.

- **Join Outdoor Clubs**: Participate in local hiking or nature groups to combine socializing with outdoor adventures.

4. Pursue Personal Development

- **Attend Workshops or Seminars**: Participate in personal development workshops, seminars, or webinars to learn new skills and meet people interested in self-growth.

- **Read Personal Development Books**: Explore books on personal growth and resilience to gain new insights and motivation.

5. Engage in Community Initiatives

- **Start a Community Project**: Initiate or join a community project or local initiative, such as a neighborhood clean-up or community garden. Contributing to a cause can foster a sense of connection and purpose.

- **Organize Social Gatherings**: Host gatherings or events, like potlucks or book clubs, to create opportunities for social interaction and build new friendships.

6. Explore Cultural Experiences

- **Attend Cultural Events**: Visit museums, theaters, or concerts to immerse yourself in cultural experiences and meet people with similar interests.

- **Learn a New Language**: Enroll in a language class to challenge yourself and connect with others who share an interest in languages and cultures.

7. Develop a New Routine

- **Create a Personal Ritual**: Establish a daily or weekly ritual that brings you joy and structure, such as a morning coffee routine, evening relaxation time, or a weekly self-care day.

- **Try a New Activity Each Week**: Commit to trying a new activity or exploring a new interest each week to keep things fresh and engaging.

8. Engage in Social Learning

- **Join a Study Group**: Participate in study groups or learning circles focused on topics you're interested in. This can be a great way to meet new people while expanding your knowledge.

- **Attend Public Lectures**: Attend public lectures or discussions on subjects you find fascinating to connect with others who share your interests.

9. Practice Mindful Eating

- **Explore Culinary Arts**: Experiment with cooking or baking new recipes. Mindful eating and exploring culinary arts can be both satisfying and a way to meet others through cooking classes or food events.

- **Join a Foodie Group**: Connect with local foodie groups or dining clubs to enjoy meals and engage in social interactions centered around food.

10. Pursue Adventure and Travel

- **Plan Mini-Adventures**: Take day trips or weekend getaways to explore new places and break out of your routine.

- **Travel Solo**: If possible, embark on solo travel experiences to gain new perspectives and build confidence.

11. Engage in Digital Detox

- **Limit Screen Time**: Reduce time spent on social media and screens to focus on in-person interactions and activities.

- **Disconnect to Reconnect**: Use the time offline to engage in activities that nurture your well-being and personal connections.

12. Embrace New Technology

- **Try Virtual Reality Experiences**: Explore virtual reality experiences to immerse yourself in new environments and activities from the comfort of home.

- **Use Social Apps Creatively**: Experiment with new social apps or platforms designed for meeting new people and fostering connections.

By incorporating these fresh approaches, you can address loneliness in innovative ways and create meaningful connections, enhancing your well-being and overall life satisfaction during and after your divorce.

CHAPTER EIGHT

The Power of Words: Mastering Communication During and After Divorce

Communicating Effectively During and After a Divorce

Going through a divorce is one of the toughest emotional experiences I've faced, and learning how to communicate in a healthy way—especially with my ex—was a journey in itself. Especially with all the pent-up anger I was still dealing with.

Whether you're talking to your former spouse, your children, in-laws, or even friends, communication can be messy, emotional, and frustrating. But it's also the key to moving forward with as much peace as possible.

Here are some things that helped me navigate those difficult conversations and might help you too:

Stay Calm and Respectful (Even When It's Hard)
There were times when I wanted to yell, cry, or say things out of anger—but I learned (sometimes the hard way) that staying calm and respectful made everything easier in the long run. When emotions run high, take a deep breath, pause, and remind yourself that reacting in anger rarely leads to the outcome you want. It's okay to walk away and return to the conversation when you feel more in control.

Be Clear and Honest
I used to sugarcoat things to avoid conflict, but I realized that being clear and direct—while still being kind—actually led to fewer misunderstandings. Say what you mean, mean what you say, and don't expect people to read between the

lines. Honest, respectful conversations help set expectations and prevent unnecessary tension.

Listen (Really Listen)
I had to learn to listen—not just wait for my turn to talk. When my ex or my kids were speaking, I made a conscious effort to hear them, not just react. Sometimes, people just want to feel understood. Nodding, making eye contact, and repeating back what you heard can make a world of difference in how a conversation unfolds.

Pick the Right Time and Place
Not every moment is the right moment for a serious conversation. I found that addressing big issues when tensions were already high—or in front of other people—made things worse. Choosing a calm, neutral setting and making sure both parties are in the right headspace can lead to more productive discussions.

Use "I" Statements Instead of Blame
Early on, I made the mistake of saying things like, "You never listen to me!" or "You always do this!"—which, unsurprisingly, put the other person on the defensive. When I started saying things like, "I feel unheard when..." or "I get frustrated when....," it changed the whole dynamic. Expressing my feelings without blame helped keep the conversation open rather than turning it into a fight.

Set Boundaries (And Stick to Them)
One of the most important lessons I learned was how to set and enforce boundaries. It's okay to decide what you will

and won't tolerate—whether that's about communication, co-parenting, or personal space. If something doesn't feel right, speak up. Boundaries aren't about controlling others; they're about protecting your own peace.

Focus on Solutions, Not Just Problems

There were plenty of times I got stuck in rehashing old arguments, but that never actually solved anything. I had to shift my focus—what can we do about this? How can we move forward? Instead of dwelling on the past, try to find solutions that work for everyone.

Stay Positive (Even When It Feels Impossible)

I won't pretend this is easy, but I found that the energy I brought to a conversation often influenced how it went. If I was defensive, the other person was too. But if I approached discussions with a calm and open mind, things tended to go much smoother. Even if the situation isn't ideal, looking for common ground can make a big difference.

Be Patient with Yourself and Others

Healing and learning to communicate effectively take time. There will be setbacks, tough days, and moments when things don't go as planned. That's okay. Progress isn't always linear. Be kind to yourself and recognize that improving communication is an ongoing process.

Get Help When You Need It

There's no shame in seeking help if communication feels impossible. I've personally benefited from therapy, mediation, and even just venting to a trusted friend. Sometimes, having a neutral third party can help bridge gaps and provide clarity when emotions make things murky.

At the end of the day, communication after divorce isn't about winning or proving a point—it's about creating a life that feels healthy and peaceful for you. Every conversation won't be perfect, and that's okay. What matters is showing up, setting boundaries, and doing your best to communicate in a way that aligns with your values.

CHAPTER NINE

Navigating Legal Challenges

LEGAL INSIGHTS: DIVORCE

Navigating legal challenges during a difficult divorce process

Understanding the legal implications of divorce proceedings is crucial.

Divorce involves a range of legal considerations, including property division, child custody, child support, and spousal support. It is important to have a basic understanding of the legal process and your rights and obligations during a divorce. Consulting with a qualified divorce attorney can help you navigate the legal aspects of the divorce and ensure that your rights are protected. Here are some key legal considerations to keep in mind during a divorce.

Grounds for divorce can differ based on where you live. Generally, there are two main types of divorce: fault and no-fault.

In a fault divorce, one party must prove that the other is responsible for the breakdown of the marriage. This could be due to reasons like adultery, abuse, or abandonment. On the other hand, a no-fault divorce doesn't require proof of any wrongdoing. It can be granted simply because the marriage is beyond repair.

The specific grounds for divorce can vary widely, including factors like living apart for a certain period or having irreconcilable differences. To understand the exact requirements and laws applicable in your area, it's essential to consult with a legal expert.

In Canada, the grounds for divorce are outlined in the Divorce Act. There are three grounds for divorce:

- Separation: You and your spouse have lived separately for at least one year and there is no reasonable prospect of reconciliation.

- Adultery: Your spouse has committed adultery and you find it intolerable to continue living together.

- Cruelty: Your spouse has treated you with physical or mental cruelty, making it intolerable to continue living together.

It's important to note that Canada has a "no-fault" divorce system, which means that you don't have to prove that your spouse was at fault for the breakdown of the marriage in order to get a divorce. The only ground that needs to be proven is the separation for at least one year.

Property Division

In most divorces, property and assets acquired during the marriage are divided between the spouses. This can be a complex and contentious issue, especially if there are significant assets involved.

In Canada, property division after a divorce is governed by the laws of the province or territory in which the couple resides.

In most cases, property acquired during the marriage is considered to be family property and is subject to equal division between the spouses upon divorce. This can include assets such as the family home, cars, bank accounts, investments, and other personal property.

There are some exceptions to the equal division rule, such as if one spouse brought significant assets into the marriage or if one spouse has been wasteful or intentionally depleted the family assets. In these cases, the court may order an unequal division of property.

Property division after a divorce is usually determined by local laws. Many jurisdictions follow one of two main systems: community property or equitable distribution. Community property means that most property acquired during the marriage is split equally between the spouses. Equitable distribution, on the other hand, divides property fairly but not necessarily equally, considering various factors such as the length of the marriage and each party's contributions.

In equitable distribution systems, property is divided based on what is considered fair under the circumstances of the marriage. This process may involve either an equal split or a distribution that takes into account factors such as each spouse's earning capacity, contributions to the marriage, and future needs.

In some jurisdictions, property acquired during the marriage is regarded as jointly owned, and each spouse is entitled to an equal share upon divorce. This principle of equal sharing ensures that assets are divided fairly, reflecting the contributions and circumstances of both parties.

Navigating Legal Challenges

The court may, however, take into account any special circumstances that would make an equal sharing of property unfair, such as the length of the marriage, the contributions of each spouse to the acquisition of the property, and the needs and obligations of each spouse. In such cases, the court may order a different division of the property.

It's important to note that property division can be a complex and contentious issue in a divorce, and it's recommended that you seek the advice of a lawyer who specializes in family law to help you navigate the process. A qualified divorce lawyer can help you understand the laws related to property division in your state or country.

Child Custody

In Chapter Four, we discussed child custody in detail. To reiterate, if you have children, one of the most important legal considerations during a divorce is determining custody.

This involves determining where the children will live, how much time they will spend with each parent, and who will make important decisions related to their upbringing. In most cases, both parents will want to maintain a close relationship with their children after the divorce, and it's important to create a custody arrangement that works for everyone involved. The specific laws and procedures related to child custody can vary depending on the jurisdiction, so it's important to consult with a qualified family law attorney for guidance. Generally speaking, child custody decisions are based on the best interests of the child, and factors such as the child's age, health, and relationship with each parent will be taken into consideration.

Child Support

Child support is a payment made by the non-custodial parent to the custodial parent to help cover the expenses of raising the child.

Child support is a legal obligation that a non-custodial parent has to provide financial assistance to the custodial parent for the care and upbringing of their child. The amount of child support can vary depending on various factors, such as the income of both parents, the needs of the child, and the custody arrangements. Child support is usually paid until the child reaches the age of majority or graduates from high school, but this can vary depending on the jurisdiction and the specific circumstances of the case.

 The amount of child support will depend on factors such as the income of the parents, the number of children involved, and the custody arrangement.

Spousal Support

Spousal support, also known as alimony, is a payment made by one spouse to the other to help support them financially after a divorce. The amount and duration of spousal support will depend on factors such as the length of the marriage, the income of both spouses, and the ability of the receiving spouse to support themselves.

Spousal support is typically awarded when one spouse has a significantly lower income or earning potential than the other spouse, and it is meant to provide financial assistance during the transition to single life or until the receiving spouse can become self-supporting.

Legal Representation

It's important to have a qualified divorce lawyer to represent you during the legal process. A good lawyer can help you understand your rights and responsibilities, negotiate with your ex-spouse, and represent you in court if necessary.

A good divorce lawyer can help you navigate the legal system, protect your interests, and achieve a fair outcome. It's important to choose a lawyer who is experienced in family law and has a good reputation in your community. You can ask for recommendations from friends and family or do your own research to find a qualified lawyer. It's also important to have open and honest communication with your lawyer so they can best represent you and your needs.

Divorce can be a complex and emotional process, and it's important to have a good understanding of your legal rights and responsibilities. Here are some tips on how to navigate the legal system and find a good lawyer:

- **Research potential lawyers:** Look for lawyers who specialize in divorce and family law. Check online reviews and ask for recommendations from friends or family members who have gone through a divorce.

- **Meet with potential lawyers:** Schedule consultations with potential lawyers to discuss your case and get a sense of their communication style and approach to divorce cases.

Finding the right lawyer for a custody case is crucial to protecting your parental rights and ensuring the best outcome for your children. Here's a step-by-step guide to help you find a qualified custody lawyer:

1. Define Your Needs

- **Assess Your Case**: Determine if your custody case is contested or uncontested, as it will influence the type of lawyer you need.

- **Consider Specializations**: Look for a lawyer specializing in family law, particularly custody cases, as they will have the expertise you require.

2. Research Potential Lawyers

- **Ask for Referrals**: Start by asking friends, family, or colleagues for recommendations if they've had a positive experience with a custody lawyer.

- **Search Online**: Use platforms like Avvo, FindLaw, or your local bar association's website to search for family lawyers in your area.

- **Check Reviews and Ratings**: Look for client reviews and ratings online to gauge a lawyer's reputation and success rate.

3. Verify Qualifications

- **Ensure Licensing**: Check that the lawyer is licensed to practice in your state or jurisdiction.

- **Experience Matters**: Look for lawyers with experience handling cases similar to yours, especially if your custody case involves unique circumstances (e.g., relocation, special needs).

- **Memberships and Awards**: Lawyers who belong to professional organizations (like the American Academy of Matrimonial Lawyers) or have received recognition for their work may be more qualified.

4. Schedule Consultations

- **Meet Multiple Lawyers**: Speak with at least three lawyers to compare their approach and expertise. Many offer free or low-cost initial consultations.

- **Prepare Questions**: Ask about:
    - ✅ Their experience with custody cases.
    - ✅ Strategies they might use for your case.
    - ✅ Expected timeline and outcomes.

☑ Fee structures (hourly rates, retainer fees, etc.).

- **Evaluate Communication**: A good lawyer will listen carefully, explain things clearly, and make you feel comfortable discussing personal matters.

5. Assess Costs

- **Understand Fees**: Lawyers may charge by the hour, require a retainer, or offer flat fees for certain services. Clarify the cost upfront to avoid surprises.

- **Weigh Value Over Price**: While affordability is important, prioritize lawyers with a proven track record, even if their rates are slightly higher.

6. Trust Your Instincts

- **Comfort Level**: Choose someone you trust and feel confident will represent your interests effectively.

- **Compatibility**: Your lawyer should align with your goals and values, especially regarding sensitive issues like custody.

7. Utilize Legal Aid if Necessary

- **Low-Cost Options**: If affordability is a concern, explore legal aid organizations, pro bono services, or lawyers who offer sliding scale fees based on income.

- **Government Resources**: Contact your local family court for referrals or legal clinics offering guidance for custody cases.

8. Finalize Your Choice
- **Review the Contract**: Carefully read the retainer agreement and clarify any doubts before signing.

- **Stay Involved**: Keep communication open with your lawyer, provide necessary documents promptly, and stay proactive in your case.

Key Considerations for Custody Cases

Focus on the child's best interests, as this is typically the court's priority.

Document everything, including communication with your ex-spouse, financial support, and interactions with your children.

Be honest and transparent with your lawyer to build a strong case.

With the right lawyer and preparation, you'll have the support needed to navigate the custody process effectively.

Understand your legal rights and responsibilities, and discuss any concerns or questions with your lawyer. Knowledge about legal considerations in a divorce is essential in making informed decisions and protecting yourself during this difficult process. Seeking the help of a qualified lawyer can also be crucial in navigating the legal aspects of divorce. Additionally, being aware of child custody and support, spousal support, and property division can aid in creating a settlement that aligns with your priorities. Overall, understanding legal considerations can provide a sense of control and empowerment during a challenging time.

Gather Necessary Documents

Collect important documents related to your marriage and financial situation to provide to your lawyer and help build your case. These documents can help your lawyer ensure that you receive a fair settlement. It's important to keep these documents organized and readily accessible to your lawyer so they can quickly access the information they need to represent you effectively. Additionally, gathering these documents early on in the process can help to streamline the divorce proceedings and minimize delays.

These documents may include:

- Marriage certificate

- Prenuptial or postnuptial agreement, if any

- Financial statements, including bank statements, credit card statements, and investment account statements

- Tax returns for the past few years

- Employment and income records for both spouses

Navigating Legal Challenges

- Property and asset ownership documents, such as deeds and titles

- Debts and liabilities records, including mortgages, loans, and credit card debts

Having all these documents in order can help your lawyer present a strong case and negotiate on your behalf during the divorce settlement process. It's important to keep them organized and easily accessible throughout the divorce proceedings.

Communicate with Your Lawyer

Stay in regular communication with your lawyer and ask questions if you don't understand something. Make sure you understand the legal process and what to expect during each stage.

Communication truly is key when working with a lawyer during a divorce. In my coaching sessions and live Facebook discussions, I always stress the importance of maintaining open and consistent communication with your lawyer. I've seen firsthand how overwhelming and confusing the legal process during a divorce can be. That's why I encourage my clients and audience to ask questions—no matter how small—whenever something isn't clear.

During my live sessions, I often share real-life examples of how failing to stay informed can lead to unnecessary stress, delays, or even unfavorable legal outcomes. I remind people that their lawyer is there to help, but it's up to them to stay engaged and proactive in their own case. I also provide practical tips on what types of questions to ask, how to organize legal documents, and how to advocate for themselves with confidence.

In my coaching, I take it a step further by helping clients identify the areas where they feel uncertain or overwhelmed in the legal process. We work together to develop strategies for clear communication with their lawyer and ensure they are fully equipped to make well-informed decisions for their future.

Ultimately, my goal is to empower people with the knowledge and confidence to navigate the legal process effectively so they don't feel lost or powerless in such an important part of their journey.

Your lawyer is there to guide you, provide clarity, and ensure you have all the necessary information to move forward confidently. Don't hesitate to voice your concerns or seek clarification about any aspect of the case. The better informed you are, the more empowered you'll feel to make decisions that align with your best interests. Your lawyer can help explain the steps involved in the divorce, from filing the initial paperwork to negotiating a settlement or representing you in court. Understanding the process can help alleviate some of the stress and uncertainty.

Consider Alternative Dispute Resolution

Consider alternative dispute resolution methods such as mediation or collaborative law, which can help you avoid lengthy court battles and potentially save money on legal fees.

Alternative dispute resolution methods such as mediation or collaborative law can be beneficial in resolving issues during a divorce without going through lengthy court battles. In mediation, a neutral third party helps the parties reach a mutually agreeable solution. In collaborative law, both parties work with their respective lawyers to resolve disputes outside of court. These methods can be less expensive and less time-consuming than going through traditional litigation, but it's important to work with a lawyer who is experienced in these methods to ensure your rights and interests are protected. Choosing alternative dispute resolution methods can often be a faster and less expensive option than traditional litigation, as it can help avoid the time and cost associated with court battles. Additionally, it can help improve communication and cooperation between the parties, which can be particularly important when children are involved.

It's important to discuss your options with your lawyer and carefully consider which method is right for your specific situation.

Focus on Your Priorities

Decide what's most important to you in the divorce settlement, and work with your lawyer to develop a strategy that aligns with your priorities.

It's essential to identify your priorities early on in the divorce process, as this can help guide your decisions and negotiations. For example, you may prioritize keeping the family home, ensuring ongoing financial support, or securing custody of your children. Once you have a clear understanding of what's most important to you, work closely with your lawyer to develop a strategy that aligns with your goals. Your lawyer can help you navigate the legal process and negotiate with your ex-spouse to achieve a settlement that meets your needs. Keep in mind that compromising on some issues may be necessary to achieve your overall goals and move forward with your life. Every divorce case is unique, and it's important to find a lawyer who understands your specific situation and can provide you with personalized guidance and support. By understanding your legal rights and responsibilities and working with a good lawyer, you can navigate the legal system with confidence and achieve a fair divorce settlement.

CHAPTER TEN

Building a Support System

In Chapters One and Two, we touched on the importance of building a support system, but I want to dive deeper into this topic because I feel so strongly about it. Divorce can be one of the most challenging and emotionally draining experiences of your life. As you navigate the complexities of legal proceedings, financial decisions, and personal upheaval, the emotional toll can often feel overwhelming. That's why having a strong support system is absolutely essential—not just as a means of surviving, but as a crucial foundation for healing and moving forward.

Why a Strong Support System Matters

Going through a divorce often triggers a cascade of intense emotions—grief, anger, sadness, confusion, and sometimes even relief. During these moments, it's easy to feel isolated, as though no one else can truly understand what you're experiencing. But this is exactly why it's so important to surround yourself with people who can provide the emotional support you need. A solid support system can help you process these emotions, offer perspective, and keep you grounded.

The role of friends and family in your healing process cannot be overstated. These individuals, who know you best, can provide empathy, understanding, and the comfort of familiar connections. However, it's important to seek out people who offer non-judgmental support—those who will listen without rushing to give advice or make you feel guilty for your feelings. Your emotions are valid, and you deserve a space where you can express yourself freely.

Seeking Professional Guidance

While friends and family are invaluable, sometimes you need a more structured form of support, especially when the emotional weight of divorce feels too heavy to carry alone. This is where professional help comes in. A therapist or counselor, particularly one with experience in divorce or family dynamics, can guide you through the emotional complexities of the process. They can offer coping strategies for managing stress, anxiety, or depression, help you process past trauma, and teach you how to build healthier emotional habits moving forward.

Therapists can also assist you in managing the grief of the end of a relationship, which is often more than just the loss of a partner—it's the loss of future plans, shared dreams, and sometimes, even a sense of identity. A professional can give you the tools to rebuild your sense of self, helping you rediscover your strengths and resilience during a time when everything may feel uncertain.

The Power of Support Groups

Sometimes, the best way to heal is by connecting with others who are walking the same path. Divorce support groups—whether in-person or online—can be a lifeline. They provide a safe, confidential environment where you can share your experiences and hear from others who understand exactly what you're going through. The sense of solidarity in these groups can be incredibly comforting. Knowing you're not alone in this journey can bring a sense of relief, and hearing how others are coping can provide fresh ideas for your own healing process.

Support groups also offer a chance to learn from others' experiences. You can gain insights into managing co-parenting challenges, dealing with difficult emotions, and navigating the changes that come with divorce. These groups often foster a sense of community that can help you feel less isolated and more empowered.

Reaching Out for Help—No Shame, Just Strength

There's no shame in needing help—whether from family, friends, a support group, or a therapist. In fact, reaching out is one of the strongest things you can do for yourself during this time. It takes courage to admit that you need support, and it takes strength to accept it when it's offered. Too often, people try to shoulder the burden of divorce on their own, but it's not something you have to face in isolation. Your healing journey will be smoother and more effective when you allow yourself to lean on others who care.

Tips for Building Your Support System

If you're unsure where to begin in building your support system, here are some actionable steps you can take:

Building a Support System

- **Reach Out to Trusted Friends and Family**: Don't be afraid to open up to those who have supported you throughout your life. Share your feelings, your struggles, and your fears. They will likely want to help, and reaching out will deepen your connection with them.

- **Join a Divorce Support Group**: Whether in person or online, connecting with others who understand your situation can be incredibly healing. You'll find compassion, empathy, and advice that can help you navigate the emotional rollercoaster of divorce.

- **Seek Professional Help**: If you're feeling overwhelmed by the emotions of divorce, don't hesitate to seek therapy or counseling. A professional can guide you through the most difficult emotions and provide valuable coping mechanisms.

- **Consider Online Support Communities**: If attending a physical support group isn't an option, look for online forums or virtual support groups. These can be great ways to connect with others from the comfort of your own home.

- **Avoid Isolation**: Even when you feel like being alone, try to stay connected with your social circle. Making an effort to spend time with loved ones, even if it's just a casual check-in, can help you avoid the emotional pitfalls of isolation.

- **Give Yourself Permission to Accept Help**: There's no need to go through this alone. Accept offers of support from those around you, whether it's help with the kids, assistance with daily tasks, or simply someone to talk to.

Remember, You're Not Alone

Divorce can feel like a long and lonely road, but it doesn't have to be. Building a strong support system is not just about getting through the legal and financial challenges; it's about preserving your emotional well-being and healing from the inside out. You are worthy of love, understanding, and support during this challenging time. Reaching out to others, whether friends, family, or professionals, is a vital step toward your healing journey.

By surrounding yourself with positive influences, leaning into support groups, and seeking professional help when necessary, you'll be able to rebuild your life stronger, more resilient, and ready to embrace the new chapter ahead. Remember, you don't have to face this alone—help is available, and it can make all the difference in your journey toward healing and recovery.

How I Built My Support System During Divorce

During my own divorce, I learned firsthand just how important it is to have a strong support system in place. In fact, the

Building a Support System

emotional weight of that experience would have been unbearable without the love and encouragement of those around me. I'd like to share some real examples of how I navigated this process and built the support I needed to heal and move forward.

Reaching Out to Close Friends and Family

At first, I tried to keep everything bottled up—thinking I should be strong and deal with it on my own. But I quickly realized that holding everything in only added to the emotional burden. I reached out to my closest friends and family members, and just having someone to talk to made a world of difference. One of my best friends, who had been through a similar experience, was a rock for me. She didn't try to fix everything but just listened when I needed to vent. She allowed me to express my feelings without judgment, and that was incredibly healing.

I also leaned on my sister, who was a steady presence throughout the process. We would talk for hours about my fears, my hopes, and the ups and downs I was experiencing. Just having someone who understood, without offering unsolicited advice, was comforting and allowed me to process my emotions at my own pace.

Joining a Divorce Support Group

I also realized that talking to people who were going through a similar experience was one of the most powerful things I could do. I joined a local divorce support group, which offered both in-person meetings and online support forums. Through these groups, I met individuals who were navigating similar challenges, and the shared experience created an instant bond. We would talk about everything—from the heartbreak of the divorce to the struggles of co-parenting to the practical steps of moving forward.

One of the things I loved most about the group was how open and honest everyone was about their struggles and triumphs. It wasn't a place for perfection—it was a place where people supported each other through the highs and lows. This group gave me a sense of community and a space where I didn't feel alone in what I was going through.

Seeking Professional Therapy and Counseling

There were times when the emotional rollercoaster of divorce became too overwhelming. I sought therapy, which was one of the best decisions I ever made. My therapist helped me understand the complex emotions I was dealing with, including anger, sadness, and guilt. She also helped me navigate the trauma that can come with divorce, not just the end of the relationship, but also the identity shift and the uncertainty of the future.

Through therapy, I learned coping strategies for managing my emotions. I was given the tools to deal with stress, anxiety, and grief in healthier ways. For example, she taught me breathing exercises to help me calm down during moments of overwhelming anxiety, and we worked on building my confidence and self-worth. Therapy helped me rediscover my inner strength and feel more in control of my life.

Online Support Communities and Forums
When I wasn't able to attend in-person group sessions due to timing or other commitments, I turned to online support groups. I found a few private Facebook groups dedicated to people going through divorce, where we could share our feelings and experiences in a safe, confidential space. It was incredibly comforting to hear stories from others who understood the emotional toll of divorce and were willing to share both their struggles and their successes.

One particular group member's post about co-parenting after divorce really resonated with me, and I reached out to her for advice. She offered some valuable insights on how to handle difficult conversations with your ex-partner and how to prioritize your children's emotional well-being. It was small exchanges like this that helped me see that there was light at the end of the tunnel, even when I felt lost.

Avoiding Isolation and Keeping Connected
There were moments when I felt like withdrawing from the world, but I pushed myself to stay connected with others. I made it a priority to have coffee dates with friends or go for walks with my sister, even on days when I felt emotionally drained. Staying engaged with people who cared about me helped me resist the temptation to isolate myself. It reminded me that I still had a support network, even on my darkest days.

One of the most memorable moments was when a dear friend took me out for a "self-care" day—something simple like a lunch and a walk in the park. It wasn't about talking about divorce; it was about restoring a sense of normalcy and giving me a break from the emotional heaviness. This small act of kindness reminded me that even during tough times, it's important to take moments to nourish myself.

Giving Myself Permission to Accept Help

During the hardest moments, I had to remind myself that it was okay to ask for help. I accepted offers from friends to help with practical tasks, like watching my kids so I could get some rest or helping me with the housework when I felt overwhelmed. Allowing myself to lean on others in this way wasn't a sign of weakness—it was a step toward healing.

One example of this was when a close friend offered to help me sort through some of my ex's things that needed to be packed away. It was a tough job, but having someone with me made it more manageable. I felt supported emotionally and physically, and I wasn't doing it alone.

The Impact of a Strong Support System

Looking back, I can see how crucial each part of my support system was. I would never have made it through without the combination of friends, family, therapy, and online support communities. Together, they helped me not only survive the divorce but also thrive afterward. They reminded me that I am worthy of love and respect and that I am capable of rebuilding my life, no matter how broken it seemed at the time.

The road to healing after divorce isn't always linear—it has its ups and downs, but with the right people around you, you can navigate those challenges with greater resilience. If I can rebuild my life after my divorce, so can you. Just remember, you don't have to do it alone—reach out, build your support system, and allow others to help guide you through. Your healing journey will be stronger, smoother, and more empowering with a solid network of people who genuinely care

CHAPTER ELEVEN

Finding Happiness and Fulfillment

Embrace life's simple pleasures, cultivate positivity, and find inner peace for true happiness.

During the divorce process, it's natural to wonder how to find happiness again. The truth is this time can be an incredible opportunity for personal growth and fulfillment—things that might have felt out of reach while you were in a marriage. Now is the perfect moment to focus on yourself, rediscover your values, and pursue the activities and relationships that bring you genuine joy. With patience, self-care, and a mindset focused on positivity, you can create a life that is not only fulfilling but also empowering. Here are some tips to help you find happiness after divorce:

- **Take time to heal and grieve:** Divorce can be a traumatic experience, and it's important to give yourself time to process your emotions and heal. Allow yourself to feel your feelings, whether it's anger, sadness, or a sense of loss.

- **Focus on your physical and mental health:** Taking care of yourself is key to finding happiness after divorce. Make sure you are eating well, exercising regularly, and getting enough rest. Consider seeing a therapist or counselor if you need support in dealing with your emotions.

- **Rediscover your passions and interests:** Use this time to explore your hobbies and interests. Rediscover what makes you happy and pursue it with passion.

- **Cultivate strong relationships:** Build and nurture relationships with friends and family. Surround yourself with positive and supportive people who will help you through this transition.

- **Embrace change and new opportunities:** Look at this as a time of opportunity. See the end of your marriage as a new beginning, a chance to create a new life for yourself that is even better than before.

Remember, happiness after divorce is possible, and it's up to you to make it happen. Stay positive, focus on self-care and growth, and keep moving forward.

More Strategies for Finding Happiness and Fulfillment After a Divorce

Going through a divorce can be an opportunity for growth and self-discovery. It can be a time to reflect on what you want in your life, set new goals, and work on personal development. This can involve exploring new hobbies, pursuing new interests, and reconnecting with yourself in a positive way. It may also involve seeking counseling or therapy to work through any emotional issues and heal from the experience. Ultimately, finding ways to use divorce as a catalyst for positive change can help you move forward in a healthy and fulfilling way. It can be a time to reflect on what you want in life and what changes you would like to make. By focusing on personal growth, you can come out of the divorce with a better understanding of yourself and your needs, which can lead to a more fulfilling life. However, it's important to remember that this process can take time and may involve seeking professional help or therapy.

Letting Go of Negative Emotions for Healthier Co-Parenting and Personal Growth

Holding on to hatred and bitterness can create a toxic environment for your children and make co-parenting more difficult. It's important to find healthy ways to manage and release any negative emotions you may have. This can include talking to a therapist, practicing self-care activities like exercise or meditation, and focusing on positive aspects of your life and future goals. Letting go of hatred can be a challenging process, but it can ultimately lead to greater emotional well-being and healthier relationships moving forward.

When you can let go of the pain and negative emotions associated with your past relationship, you can focus on being the best parent possible for your children. This means working with your ex-partner to provide a stable and supportive environment for your children, even if you are no longer together as a couple. This can be challenging, but it's important to prioritize your children's well-being and put your differences aside for their sake. With time and effort, it's possible to build a positive co-parenting relationship and provide your children with the love and support they need to thrive.

However, it's important to reflect on the reasons why the marriage didn't work out to avoid making the same mistakes

Finding Happiness and Fulfillment

in future relationships. Take the time to think about what you want and need in a partner and a relationship. This self-reflection can help you move forward and make positive changes in your life.

While it is important not to dwell on the past, it is essential to remember why you got divorced in the first place. Often, when you are no longer in a bad marriage, the negative experiences fade away. Along with helping you build healthier relationships moving forward, reflecting on what went wrong can also give you a sense of closure and allow you to move on with your life in a positive way.

Of course, this is easier said than done, especially depending on the severity of the trauma you endured. This is another area where a strong support structure and mental health professional can be helpful.

It is natural to miss someone you shared a big part of your life with. However, there are reasons you got divorced, especially if you left a narcissist. Divorce is usually the result of serious issues in a marriage, and leaving a narcissistic partner can be especially challenging. Narcissistic partners can be emotionally manipulative and abusive, and leaving such a relationship can be a step towards protecting your mental health and well-being. If you find yourself struggling to move on after leaving a narcissistic partner, seeking support from a therapist or counselor can be helpful in the healing process.

Leaving a toxic relationship, especially with a narcissist, is often the best decision for your well-being and safety. While it's natural to feel sadness or nostalgia for the good times, it's important to remind yourself of the reasons you chose to leave and the negative impact the relationship had on your life. By focusing on the present and building a brighter future for yourself, you can move forward and find happiness.

Discover Yourself

Getting over your divorce is a process that involves self-discovery. As a married person, you shared a lot with your spouse—your dreams, your challenges, your joys, and your vulnerabilities. You built a life together, created memories, and intertwined your goals and hopes for the future. However, when a marriage ends, it's natural to feel a sense of loss as these shared experiences no longer have the same place in your life. It's important to acknowledge the significance of those memories while also recognizing that your journey moving forward is now one of personal growth and rediscovery. Letting go of the past can be difficult, but it opens up the space to focus on your own needs, desires, and aspirations. This is a time for you to reclaim your individuality and focus on what truly makes you happy, without the constraints of the past. While the shared experiences may have defined a chapter of your life, the next chapter is yours to write—with new opportunities, new relationships, and a renewed sense of purpose. To move on and create a happy life after divorce, it's essential to rediscover who you are as an individual. Take some time to explore your interests, hobbies, and passions. Consider trying new things or revisiting old ones that you may have set aside during your marriage.

Take the time to reflect on your values, beliefs, and personal goals. Ask yourself what kind of life you want to lead and what steps you can take to achieve your dreams. By discovering your authentic self and what truly makes you happy, you can build a fulfilling life post-divorce.

Identify your values: Take some time to reflect on your values and what's most important to you. This could include things like family, health, career, personal growth, or spirituality. By identifying your values, you can create a roadmap for building a life that aligns with your priorities.

Set goals: Once you've identified your values, set some specific goals that align with those values. These could be short-term or long-term goals, and they could be related to your career, relationships, health, or personal growth. Setting goals gives you a sense of purpose and direction, and helps you focus your energy on the things that matter most to you.

Pursue your passions and interests: Use this time to explore your passions and interests. What do you love to do? What activities make you feel most alive and engaged? Whether it's taking a cooking class, joining a hiking group, or volunteering for a cause you're passionate about, pursuing your interests can help you find meaning and fulfillment in life.

Surround yourself with positivity: Surround yourself with positive people who support and uplift you. Cultivate relationships with people who share your values and inspire you to be your best self.

Practice gratitude: Practicing gratitude can help you cultivate a positive mindset and appreciate the good things in your life. Take time each day to reflect on what you're grateful for and focus on the positives, even during challenging times.

Make it a point to get outside of your comfort zone and do things you've never done before. Doing things for the first time will help build your confidence and allow you to get to know yourself better.

You may find that you have talents or interests that you never knew you had. This can also be a great way to meet new people and build new relationships. Consider trying activities such as hiking, taking a dance class, volunteering, or traveling to a new place.

Stepping out of your comfort zone can be scary, but it can also be incredibly rewarding. It's when you push past your fears and embrace new challenges that you unlock your true potential. By taking risks, whether big or small, you open yourself up to new experiences, growth, and self-discovery. Although the unfamiliar may feel daunting at first, it often leads to unexpected opportunities and a stronger sense of confidence. Each time you step outside what feels safe, you expand your horizons and gain the courage to face even greater challenges ahead. The rewards—whether personal, professional, or emotional—are worth the discomfort, and they pave the way for a more fulfilling life.

Remember, finding happiness and fulfillment after a divorce is a journey, not a destination. It takes time, effort, and

Finding Happiness and Fulfillment

self-reflection to create a life that aligns with your values and brings you joy. But by taking small steps every day and staying true to yourself, you can create a fulfilling and rewarding life after divorce. *Don't rush into a new relationship.*

Rushing into a new relationship too soon after your divorce can lead to more heartache. If things do not work out in your new relationship, it adds insult to injury.

It does not mean you have to give up on love. Just take some time to figure out what you want in your post-divorce life. There is nothing wrong with being single.

If the right person comes along, they will understand you taking some time before jumping into anything. Take things slowly, especially if it's your first time dating again after an unhappy marriage.

This can help you avoid a future divorce.

Keep in mind that negative people prey on the vulnerable, so if someone is overly pushy about entering into a new relationship, that might be a warning sign. This behavior can be a sign of manipulation, not genuine connection. Trust your instincts and take the time to truly assess whether their intentions align with your well-being. It's crucial to protect your heart and guard against those who seek to exploit your openness.

Give It Time

You have to expect that it will take some time to adjust to life after your divorce. Do not expect things to be outstanding immediately.

If you do not plan for the adjustment period, it can catch you off guard and make things more difficult. Just remember that it takes time to start your new life and find your own happiness.

It's important to have realistic expectations and allow yourself time to adjust to your new life. Give yourself the space to grieve and process your emotions. Remember that healing is a process, and it's okay to take things one day at a time.

It's important to be patient with yourself and allow yourself time to adjust to your new reality. Divorce can be a major life change, and it's normal to experience a range of emotions, including sadness, anger, and confusion. Give yourself permission to feel these emotions and take the time you need to process them.

CHAPTER TWELVE

Creating a Positive Co-Parenting Relationship

Navigating Co-Parenting After Divorce: My Personal Experience and Key Strategies

Co-parenting after divorce is one of the hardest things I've had to navigate. Even after custody arrangements were settled, the challenges didn't just disappear. Emotions were still raw, disagreements still surfaced, and learning how to co-exist as parents—without being partners—was a process that took time and patience.

I remember times when simple scheduling changes would turn into heated debates or when differences in parenting styles made me question whether we'd ever find common ground. There were moments of frustration, anger, and even guilt—wondering if my children were being affected by the tension. And the truth is, they were. Experiencing this firsthand with my own children made me realize the importance of adjusting my approach to co-parenting. I saw how my choices and interactions directly impacted them, which led me to rethink how I handled communication, boundaries, and cooperation with my ex to create a healthier environment for everyone involved.

The turning point for me was understanding that no matter how I felt about my ex, my children deserved peace, stability, and a home environment where they weren't caught in the middle. I had to shift my mindset from lingering on past grievances to focusing on what was best for them. This meant choosing cooperation over conflict, even when it was difficult.

Creating a Positive Co-Parenting Relationship

Here's what helped me navigate co-parenting in a healthier, more productive way:

- ✅ Keeping Communication Business-Like – Instead of engaging emotionally, I started treating conversations with my ex as I would a professional exchange. Keeping things clear, direct, and respectful helped minimize unnecessary arguments.

- ✅ Picking My Battles – Not everything needed to turn into a dispute. I learned to ask myself, "Is this about control, or is this truly about what's best for the kids?" If it was the latter, I addressed it. If it wasn't, I let it go.

- ✅ Creating Consistency for the Kids – Whether it was routines, house rules, or expectations, I found that the more consistency we maintained between households, the more secure my children felt.

- ✅ Focusing on What I Could Control – I couldn't change my ex's parenting style, but I could control how I responded and how I showed up for my children. Shifting my energy away from frustration and toward creating a loving, stable environment in my own home made a huge difference.

- ✅ Using an App – To reduce misunderstandings and keep everything organized, we started using a co-parenting app for schedules, expenses, and communication. This took a lot of stress out of coordinating things.

I won't pretend that co-parenting magically became easy, but over time, I saw the impact these changes had on my children. They became more relaxed and more open, and they no longer felt like they had to choose sides.

At the end of the day, co-parenting isn't about winning or losing—it's about making choices that allow your children to grow up in an environment of respect, love, and stability. If you're struggling with co-parenting, I encourage you to focus on what's within your control, set clear boundaries, and always keep your children's well-being at the center of every decision. It won't be perfect, but small changes can make a big difference.

Use Clear and Non-Defensive Communication

Effective communication is the foundation of conflict resolution. It's essential to express yourself in a way that encourages understanding rather than escalating tension. One of the most powerful tools in non-defensive communication is the use of "I" statements.

Instead of saying "You always ignore my input," try saying, "I feel frustrated when I don't feel heard in our discussions." This subtle shift takes the focus off the other person's behavior and centers it on your feelings, which reduces the likelihood of defensiveness. By expressing your emotions and needs clearly, without blaming or accusing, you create a space for open dialogue rather than escalating conflict.

Listen Actively and Patiently

Conflict resolution is not just about speaking your truth; it's about listening with the intent to understand. When disagreements arise, it's important to listen carefully to the other person's perspective before jumping in with your response. Active listening means truly focusing on what the other person is saying without formulating a rebuttal in your mind while they're speaking.

Give the other person your full attention and allow them to express their thoughts without interruption. This simple act shows respect and allows for clearer communication, ultimately making it easier to find common ground. When you feel heard, you are more likely to be receptive to hearing the other person's side.

Respect the Other Person's Point of View

In any conflict, both parties may have valid concerns, but it's easy to get caught up in wanting to prove you're right. To resolve conflicts effectively, it's essential to approach the situation with empathy and respect for the other person's perspective. This doesn't mean you need to agree on everything, but it does mean acknowledging their feelings and viewpoint.

Try to see the issue from their perspective—whether it's a decision about the children's education, discipline, or scheduling. This can help de-escalate the situation and demonstrate that you value the other parent's input, which fosters a cooperative dynamic in your co-parenting relationship.

Stay Calm and Composed

When emotions run high, it's easy to lose control and say things that you may regret later. Staying calm in the face of conflict is one of the most important strategies for managing disagreements effectively. If you feel yourself becoming angry or upset, it's okay to take a pause. Step back from the conversation, take deep breaths, and allow yourself time to cool down before continuing.

During moments of heightened emotion, taking a break can be an incredibly powerful way to prevent the situation from escalating. It also allows both parties the space to collect their thoughts and return to the conversation in a more composed and rational state.

Avoid Criticism and Focus on Solutions

Criticism can easily derail a productive conversation and lead to defensiveness and resentment. Instead of criticizing the other person's behavior, ideas, or decisions, focus on what can be changed in a positive, collaborative way.

For example, instead of saying, "You never take my concerns seriously," try framing your thoughts with a focus on what you would like to see change: "I feel that my concerns about the children's schooling are not being fully addressed. Can we work together to ensure we are both involved in their educational decisions?" By focusing on solutions rather than pointing out flaws, you create a more constructive environment that encourages compromise and cooperation.

Co-Parenting with Mutual Respect

Co-parenting isn't always easy, but it plays a crucial role in your child's well-being after a divorce or separation. When parents find ways to resolve conflicts in a healthy and respectful manner, children are less likely to feel the emotional strain of their parents' disagreements. On the other hand, when conflict remains unresolved or becomes hostile, children can experience confusion, stress, and even feelings of guilt, believing they are somehow responsible for the tension.

A strong co-parenting relationship reassures children that, despite the changes in their family, they are still loved and supported by both parents. When parents work together, make important decisions as a team, and present a united front, they create a sense of stability that helps children feel secure and emotionally grounded.

It's important to recognize that the way parents handle conflict doesn't just affect their own relationship—it directly impacts how their child processes and adjusts to the changes in their family dynamics. By staying calm, focusing on solutions instead of past grievances, and prioritizing the child's well-being above all else, co-parents can create an environment where their child feels safe, supported, and free to thrive.

In my own experience, co-parenting required me to navigate not only the relationship with my ex-husband but also with my in-laws. This dynamic added an extra layer of complexity, but over time, I learned that it was important to prioritize the well-being of our children and maintain a collaborative approach, even when it wasn't always easy.

When my children were younger, I found myself in a situation where I had to find a way to ensure they were well taken care of after school while I was at work. Instead of letting the tension between myself and my ex or the difficulties with our relationship get in the way, I made a decision that ultimately supported my children and provided them with stability. I moved into a house on the next street from my in-laws so that they could help out by babysitting the children after school until I was able to get home from work.

At first, this wasn't an easy decision. The idea of being so close to my ex-husband's family, especially when we were still adjusting to the changes in our family, felt overwhelming. But I realized that this arrangement provided my children with continuity—they were familiar with their grandparents, and it also allowed me to manage my work and personal commitments more effectively. Most importantly, it made sure that my children weren't left alone or feeling like they had to adjust to too many changes all at once.

Although I was nervous at first about managing the emotional complexity of being so close to my in-laws after everything that had transpired, I made sure to set clear boundaries. I communicated openly with them about my needs and expectations. I was clear about my role as my children's mother and what I wanted in terms of their involvement in our children's lives, while also respecting their role as grandparents. It was crucial to maintain a

Creating a Positive Co-Parenting Relationship

balance between allowing them to play an active role in the children's lives without letting it interfere with my autonomy as a parent.

This arrangement worked surprisingly well. My children thrived knowing they had a safe, familiar place to go after school, and I could focus on my job knowing they were in good hands. Over time, it also helped to foster a more amicable relationship with my in-laws. We weren't perfect, but we found a way to work together for the benefit of the kids, which is what ultimately mattered most.

There were challenges, of course. There were times when boundaries were tested, emotions ran high, and misunderstandings arose. But through patience, mutual respect, and keeping the focus on the needs of the children, we made it work. It wasn't always smooth, but the key was communication and understanding that we were all working toward the same goal: giving our children a stable, loving environment, despite the changes in our family structure.

Ultimately, this experience taught me that co-parenting doesn't always follow a traditional path. Sometimes, the support system you need might come from unexpected places, and the willingness to be flexible and put the kids' needs first can make all the difference in creating a nurturing environment for them.

Other positive coparenting practices include:

Doing what is in the best interest of the child when handling decisions: Putting the best interests of the child first should always be the top priority for parents, both during and after a divorce. This means making decisions that prioritize the child's well-being and emotional health, such as agreeing on a co-parenting plan that allows the child to spend quality time with both parents, attending important events and appointments, and communicating with each other respectfully about the child's needs and concerns. When both parents work together to prioritize the child's best interests, the child is more likely to thrive and feel secure.

Respecting the other parent's right to participate in parenting practices: Respecting the other parent's right to participate in parenting practices is an important aspect of co-parenting. Both parents should have an equal say in important decisions regarding their child's upbringing and well-being. It is important to communicate effectively and work together to find solutions that are in the best interest of the child. Avoiding negative comments or actions towards the other parent can also help maintain a positive co-parenting relationship.

Agreeing on some basic rules for raising the children: Yes, agreeing on some basic rules for raising children can be very helpful in co-parenting after divorce. This can include things like agreeing on bedtimes, homework schedules, screen time limits, discipline strategies, and more. Having these basic rules in place can help provide consistency and stability for children as they navigate their new family dynamic. It can also help prevent disagreements between co-parents and provide a clear understanding of expectations. By agreeing on basic rules for raising their children, both parents can work together to provide a stable and consistent environment for their children, which can help them adjust to the changes brought on by the divorce. This can include things like bedtime routines, screen time limits, discipline practices, and more. It is important for both parents to be on the same page about these rules to avoid confusion and inconsistency for the children.

Letting go of feelings of anger and resentment: It is important for both parents to let go of any feelings of anger and resentment towards each other, as these emotions can negatively affect their ability to co-parent effectively. This may involve seeking therapy or counseling to work through these emotions and find healthy ways to cope with them. It is also important to communicate openly and respectfully with the other parent, focusing on the needs and well-being of the children.

Holding on to negative emotions can lead to tension and conflict, which can ultimately harm the children's well-being and emotional health. Learning to forgive and move on can help create a more positive and healthy co-parenting relationship.

Co-parenting after a divorce can be challenging, but it's important to prioritize your children's needs and create a positive co-parenting relationship with your ex-spouse. Here are some strategies to help you build a healthy co-parenting relationship:

Prioritize your children's needs: Your children should always come first. Focus on their well-being and make decisions that are in their best interest.

Communicate effectively: Communication is key to a successful co-parenting relationship. Be respectful and clear in your communication and try to keep emotions in check. Consider using a neutral mode of communication like email or a co-parenting app.

Build trust: Trust is essential in any relationship, including co-parenting. Keep your promises, show up on time, and be reliable. This will help build trust and create a more positive co-parenting dynamic.

Show respect: Respect your ex-spouse's opinions and decisions, even if you don't agree with them. Remember, you both have the same goal: to raise happy, healthy children.

Be flexible: Co-parenting requires flexibility and compromise. Be open to your ex-spouse's schedule and needs, and try to work together to create a parenting plan that works for everyone.

Seek support: Co-parenting can be stressful and emotional. Consider seeking support from a therapist, support group, or trusted friend or family member to help you cope with the challenges.

Creating a Positive Co-Parenting Relationship

Remember, creating a positive co-parenting relationship takes time and effort. By prioritizing your children's needs, communicating effectively, and showing respect and flexibility, you can build a healthy co-parenting relationship with your ex-spouse.

CHAPTER THIRTEEN

Overcoming Shame and Stigma

RISING FROM DIVORCE'S ASHES

"Embrace your journey. Divorce does not define you; it refines you into a stronger soul."

Overcoming Shame and Stigma

Divorce often brings with it an overwhelming sense of shame and the weight of societal judgment. The expectation that marriage should last a lifetime, paired with cultural narratives that view divorce as a failure, can make it hard to embrace the reality of your situation. However, it is crucial to understand that divorce is not a reflection of your worth as a person—it's a decision that many people face, and sometimes it's the healthiest choice for all involved.

Rather than internalizing the shame society may impose, it's vital to reframe your perspective. Divorce may be the end of a relationship, but it is not the end of your value, nor does it diminish your future potential. Overcoming the stigma attached to divorce involves recognizing the complexities of your journey and giving yourself the grace to heal, grow, and redefine your path forward.

Is It Selfish or Frivolous to Care About Your Self-Esteem During a Divorce?

It is neither selfish nor frivolous to prioritize your self-esteem during a divorce. In fact, it is essential. Divorce is an emotional upheaval, and the process can chip away at your confidence, leaving you questioning your sense of identity and worth. Acknowledging and addressing your emotional well-being during this time is a vital part of healing.

Self-esteem is the foundation of resilience. It helps you navigate the emotional challenges of divorce, giving you the strength to move forward with confidence. Instead of letting the divorce define you, take proactive steps to nurture and rebuild your self-worth. This is not an indulgence—it is necessary for your healing and growth.

Engage in practices that promote self-care, whether that's investing time in activities that bring you joy, seeking therapy, or surrounding yourself with a supportive network of friends and family. Make time for hobbies, self-reflection, and activities that reestablish a sense of purpose and fulfillment. By prioritizing your emotional health and self-esteem, you not only equip yourself to handle the challenges of divorce but also set the stage for a future of personal growth and resilience.

Remember, your worth is not defined by the end of a relationship; it's defined by your ability to rise, learn, and continue moving forward, stronger than before.

The Importance of Self-Esteem

Building self-esteem strengthens your ability to handle the emotional toll of divorce while also giving you the inner resources to support your children, if you have them. When you cultivate a strong sense of self-worth, it's like planting a tree—one person's growth can inspire and positively impact those around them. And if enough people do the same, the entire environment becomes healthier, creating a ripple effect of strength, confidence, and emotional well-being.

Evaluating Self-Esteem Before the Divorce

If you are going through a divorce, it can be helpful to evaluate your self-esteem before the divorce. If your self-esteem was already low, the divorce process might exacerbate those feelings. On the other hand, if your self-esteem was high, it may help you cope better with the stress and challenges of the divorce process. Evaluating your self-esteem can help you identify areas for improvement and give you the opportunity to work on building your self-esteem during and after the divorce.

Self-Esteem Before Marriage

What was your self-esteem like going into the marriage? Your baseline level of self-esteem will affect how you experience divorce far more than the other way around. If you've experienced low self-esteem throughout your life, divorce is likely to be more devastating, and healing could take longer. Low self-esteem will also make it more likely that you'll struggle with managing your kids', friends', or relatives' reactions, and that you'll place excessive blame on yourself, your partner, or both. Managing emotions and dealing with blame are challenging enough without the complication of low self-esteem.

Building Self-Esteem Before or During Divorce

Begin by recognizing the difference between genuine self-esteem and an ego boost. Both feel great, but there are differences. An ego boost is created by external things like a new relationship, a good grade, or driving a nice car. Self-esteem, on the other hand, is an inside job, resulting from accepting and embracing your authentic self. With an ego boost, as soon as the external factor is gone, so is the good feeling. Ego boosts are temporary, but your baseline level of self-esteem is always with you.

Accepting your feelings and acknowledging that they matter is crucial for boosting your self-esteem. Fighting or struggling with difficult feelings only adds to the pain. Give in to the "ugly" feelings sometimes; honoring your feelings honors you. Note that "giving in" does not mean "acting on" them. Just let yourself have your feelings, acknowledge and label them. No one else has to know that you're allowing yourself to have your feelings—it's your little secret.

Allowing Yourself to Feel

For example, if you're home alone and suddenly remember the beginning of your relationship—all those hopes for a bright future—and feel a wave of sadness, allow yourself to feel it. Instead of distracting yourself, let the tears come if they want to. Feel the sadness, remember the good times, and acknowledge your loss. The immediate experience of the feeling will subside eventually. Trust the process. Allowing yourself to feel enhances self-esteem by providing a sense of your own humanity and wholeness.

Self-Esteem Fluctuations

Yes, self-esteem can fluctuate over time, influenced by many factors such as life experiences, relationships, and personal achievements. It is normal to have fluctuations in self-esteem, and it's important to work on building a healthy sense of self-worth and confidence over time.

Increasing Self-Esteem

Rather than trying to feel good about yourself and everything you do—which merely means you're attempting to fool yourself—make a pledge to become aware of your thoughts, feelings, and behavior. When you have low self-esteem, awareness is your enemy. There are things you just don't want to know about yourself because it feels too dangerous. Embracing awareness offers great rewards. Aim to make clear-eyed awareness your friend, and watch your integrity and self-esteem improve.

Be honest with yourself about how you contributed to the dissolution of your marriage. Allow yourself to grieve the loss of your relationship or admit to feeling relieved about the divorce. You don't have to tell the kids, but it's very important that you acknowledge your true feelings to yourself.

Protecting Your Kids' Self-Esteem

The number one thing you can do to protect your kids' self-esteem is to ensure they understand they are not at fault for the divorce. Tell them and show them in as many ways as you can that they are loved and cherished as much as ever. They need a consistently repeated message to inoculate them against doubt.

Let them know it's okay to talk about the divorce. Your challenge is to be okay with your kids expressing their feelings, thoughts, and observations. If you disagree with them, say so; but don't ask them not to talk about it. They need your help to process their feelings.

Lastly, make your own choices and don't make your kid responsible for grown-up decisions. They are along for the ride, not driving the bus—try to make it as smooth and comfortable for them as possible. Do not let them take care of you, but let them know explicitly that you love them as much as ever.

> *"Your value doesn't decrease based on someone's inability to see your worth." – Unknown*

Do You Know Your Worth?

Self-worth is how you value yourself.

Our sense of worth doesn't stem from external judgments or our achievements (or lack thereof)—it comes from within.

However, it's easy to forget that our true value isn't defined by outside influences.

We often gauge our self-worth without even realizing how we do it. Sometimes we measure it by our careers, our appearance, or our relationships—comparing this to measuring our height with an arbitrary stick.

The reality is, we frequently assess our worth, but we don't always recognize how we're doing it.

When it comes to measuring self-worth, many people rely on something just as unpredictable as an arbitrary stick. You may not consciously choose the method of measurement, but deep down, you likely know it. After all, when you feel like you're meeting the mark, your confidence soars. But when you feel like you've fallen short, your self-esteem can take a dive.

Too often, the "stick" we use to assess our value is beyond our control. We base our self-worth on things like checking off items on a to-do list, getting matches on a dating app, receiving likes on a social media post, or earning promotions—the list can seem endless. We tend to feel the impact of our worth calculations (like those moments of "I'm not good enough"), but rarely do we pause to reflect on how we're measuring ourselves in the first place.

We often notice how our sense of self-worth impacts our emotions, yet we rarely pause to reflect on how we are measuring it.

Overcoming Shame and Stigma

I've learned that the way we see ourselves shapes every aspect of our lives. For years, I let external factors—other people's opinions, life circumstances, and even past experiences—define my worth. And when things didn't go the way I hoped, whether it was a failed relationship or a setback in my career, my self-esteem took a hit. It felt like I was constantly riding an emotional rollercoaster, where my confidence depended on things I couldn't control.

But the truth is, our value isn't something that should be determined by others or by life's unpredictable twists and turns. The only true measure of self-worth is the one we set for ourselves. When I started focusing on what I could control—my growth, my character, my integrity—I stopped feeling like a victim of circumstance.

Life will always have ups and downs. You might lose a job, go through a divorce, or face rejection, but when you truly know who you are and appreciate the person you've become, those setbacks won't shake you. Instead of questioning your worth, you'll trust yourself to navigate the challenges, knowing that your value isn't tied to what happens to you—it's rooted in who you are.

I had to learn this lesson the hard way. For most of my life, I was a people pleaser, believing that my worth was measured by how much I could do for others. I constantly felt the need to prove myself, to keep everyone happy—even if it meant sacrificing my own happiness. I bent over backward, saying yes when I wanted to say no, putting everyone else first until I hardly recognized myself anymore. In trying so hard to be what others needed, I lost sight of who I was and what truly mattered to me.

Fortunately, I've come to realize that using this "measuring stick" only led to disappointment. I decided that my happiness mattered more than trying to meet others' expectations. Though I'm still growing, I now try to assess my worth based on my own sense of self, rather than how others see me. Instead of chasing external validation, focus on measuring your self-worth by the person you are at your core.

When you need a reminder to detach from external measures of self-worth, here's a list of things that don't define your value in this world.

15 Things That *Don't* Determine Your Self-Worth

- **Your To-Do List:** I used to measure my value by how much I accomplished in a day. If I wasn't constantly checking off tasks, I felt like I wasn't enough. But I've learned that self-worth isn't about productivity—it's about who you are at your core. You are valuable even on the days when you don't get everything done.

- **Your Job:** Your job is just one part of your life—it's not who you are. I've had jobs that made me feel important and others that made me feel invisible, but neither changed my worth. Whether you're at the top of your career or figuring things out, your value remains the same.

- **Your Social Media Following:** It's easy to fall into the trap of thinking that more likes or followers mean you matter more. I've been there. But social media is just a highlight reel, and your worth isn't tied to numbers on a screen. The most important connections are the ones that exist offline.

- **Your Age:** For so long, I thought I had to hit certain milestones by a certain age—marriage, kids, career success. But life doesn't work that way. Your worth doesn't decrease because you're getting older or because you're not "where you should be." You are valuable at every stage, every season, every moment.

- **Your Appearance:** I've changed my look many times—new hair, new clothes, weight loss, weight gain—thinking it would make me feel worthy. And sure, sometimes it gave me a boost, but real confidence doesn't come from the mirror. Looks change, but who you are—your kindness, your strength, your heart—that's what lasts.

- **Other People:** It's so tempting to compare yourself to others, but I've learned that we're all on different journeys. Someone else's success, beauty, or happiness doesn't take away from your own. Stay in your lane, focus on your path, and know that you are enough, just as you are.

- **Your Fitness Level:** I used to think I had to reach a certain weight or fitness goal to feel good about myself. But self-worth isn't about how far you can run, how much you can lift, or what size jeans you wear. It's about taking care of yourself in a way that feels good—not punishing yourself for not being "perfect."

- **Your Achievements:** I used to believe that success meant being the best, getting the highest grades, and constantly proving myself. But life isn't a report card. You are not defined by numbers, titles, or trophies. You matter simply because you exist.

- **The Number of Friends You Have:** For a long time, I thought my worth was tied to how many people liked me. But it's not about numbers—it's about quality. A few real, supportive friendships are worth more than a thousand shallow connections.

- **Your Relationship Status:** Being single doesn't mean you're unworthy of love. I've been there—feeling like I needed to be in a relationship to feel valuable. But I've learned that the most important relationship is the one you have with yourself. You are whole, with or without a partner.

- **Your Bank Account:** Money can make life easier, but it doesn't determine your worth. I've been in tough financial situations, and I've had times when I was comfortable—but neither changed who I am as a person. Your kindness, integrity, and heart matter more than any dollar amount.

- **Your Interests and Passions:** Love what you love, even if it's not "cool" or trendy. Whether it's the music you listen to, the books you read, or the hobbies you enjoy, those things make you you. And that's something to celebrate, not hide.

- **What Other People Think:** For years, I let other people's opinions shape how I saw myself. But I've learned that no one else gets to decide my worth—I do. And so do you. What you think about yourself is what matters most.

- **Your Past Mistakes**: I've made mistakes—big ones. But I am not my past, and neither are you. Every mistake is just a lesson, a stepping stone, not a life sentence. What defines you is how you rise, learn, and grow.

- **What You Own:** I used to think that having the right clothes, the right car, or the right house meant I had "made it." But none of those things bring real fulfillment. At the end of the day, what truly matters is who you are, not what you own.

Your worth isn't something you have to earn. It's already yours. You are enough—always.

Here are some strategies to help you overcome feelings of shame and stigma related to divorce:

Reframe your thinking: Challenge negative self-talk and reframe your thinking to focus on your strengths and positive qualities. Remind yourself that divorce does not define you and that you are still a valuable and worthy person.

Seek support: Surround yourself with people who support and encourage you. This could include friends, family members, or a support group for people going through divorce. Talking to others who have been through similar experiences can help you feel less alone and more validated.

Practice self-compassion: Be kind to yourself and practice self-compassion. Treat yourself with the same kindness and understanding that you would offer a close friend going through a difficult time. Recognize that divorce is a challenging process, and it's okay to feel a range of emotions.

Educate yourself: Learn more about divorce and the common challenges people face during the process. Understanding the common experiences and emotions associated with divorce can help you feel less alone and more empowered.

Focus on personal growth: Use this time as an opportunity for personal growth and self-discovery. Explore new interests, hobbies, or skills that you've always wanted to try. By focusing on your own personal growth, you can build a positive self-image and a sense of confidence and independence.

Divorce is a difficult process, and it's normal to feel a range of emotions, including shame. By reframing your thinking, seeking support, practicing self-compassion, educating yourself, and focusing on personal growth, you can overcome shame and stigma and build a positive self-image.

CHAPTER FOURTEEN

Redefining Your Relationships

When I first watched *The War of the Roses* in the late 1980s, divorce wasn't even a concept I had seriously considered, let alone the venomous battles that can accompany it. Back then, I was in a completely different place in my life—a hopeful, idealistic version of myself who saw marriage as a partnership that could weather any storm. I went to see this movie, expecting a dark comedy, something outrageous and exaggerated, a piece of entertainment far removed from my own reality. And at the time, that's exactly what I thought it was.

I remember being both horrified and amused by Michael Douglas and Kathleen Turner's explosive performances as Oliver and Barbara Rose. Their descent into marital warfare was shocking, to say the least, but it felt so extreme, almost cartoonish in its absurdity. From sabotaged dinners to demolished chandeliers, the sheer audacity of their antics made me laugh nervously, thankful that such a scenario felt like something out of fiction rather than a mirror to my own life.

I couldn't help but think, "How could two people who once loved each other this much get to such a hateful place?" I chalked it up to Hollywood exaggeration, a clever satire of materialism and ego. The Roses weren't just fighting over a house; they were dismantling their lives brick by brick, piece by piece. At the time, it seemed so far-fetched—dramatic entertainment with no bearing on my own quiet, stable marriage.

Danny DeVito's narration as the Roses' lawyer, Gavin D'Amato, felt like a warning to others: *Don't let this happen to you.* He was the voice of reason amidst the chaos, telling the story with both humor and an underlying sadness. I left the theater entertained, slightly uneasy, but mostly thinking, "Thank goodness this isn't my reality." I thought the Roses' obsession with winning—no matter the cost—was ridiculous, something that could never happen to real people, let alone me.

But now, years later, looking back, the movie hits me differently. Life has a way of surprising you, doesn't it? I never imagined I'd one day find myself navigating the emotional and legal battles of a divorce—let alone the custody fights, the hurtful words, and the feeling of being locked in a war with someone I once loved. The Roses' story, which once felt so over-the-top, now feels painfully real in hindsight.

When I think about Barbara's character, I see a woman who started as a devoted wife but slowly lost herself, her voice drowned out by Oliver's ambitions. And Oliver? He wasn't a monster—he was a man who believed he was doing what was best for them, blind to how he was diminishing Barbara's sense of independence and worth. Their tragedy wasn't that they fought; it was that they stopped communicating and allowed their anger to fester. Watching the movie now, I can see that the seeds of their destruction were planted long before the first fight over the house.

Back in the '80s, I couldn't relate to the idea of a marriage crumbling so spectacularly. Today, though, I can see how small resentments, unspoken frustrations, and a refusal to compromise can build into something unmanageable.

The house they fought over—the symbol of their success—became the battlefield for their anger. And isn't that what happens sometimes in real life? The things you build together, the things you cherish, can become weapons when love turns to resentment.

The movie's dark humor and satire hit differently now, too. In the '80s, I laughed at their ridiculous antics, but today, I wince at the truth beneath the comedy. The laughter has a bitter edge, not because the movie has changed, but because my perspective has. Back then, I saw *The War of the Roses* as a cautionary tale about letting materialism and pride rule a relationship. Now, I see it as a much deeper warning: Nurture your relationships, communicate, and don't let resentment take root.

I still think the movie is brilliant. The performances are stellar—Michael Douglas and Kathleen Turner bring both charm and venom to their roles, and Danny DeVito's direction keeps the tone perfectly balanced between comedy and tragedy. But watching it now, after having lived through my own version of those kinds of emotional battles, I feel the weight of its message more profoundly.

In a way, I'm grateful I saw it when I did, back when divorce was something that happened to other people. At the time, it planted a small seed of awareness, even if I didn't realize it. And now, looking back, *The War of the Roses* feels less like an exaggerated satire and more like a stark reminder of how quickly love can turn if we're not careful.

Redefining Your Relationships

If I could go back to that younger version of myself sitting in the theater, I'd tell her to pay closer attention—not just to the movie but to her own life. I'd remind her that love needs care, that marriage requires communication, and that pride is rarely worth the cost. Because while the movie may be outrageous, the emotions behind it are very real, and the lessons it offers are ones I've learned the hard way.

In the end, *The War of the Roses* isn't just a dark comedy; it's a deeply human story about what can happen when love turns to hate. Watching it now, with the weight of my own experiences, it's both harder to watch and more meaningful than ever.

When a marriage ends, one of the hardest realizations is accepting that you may never get the answers, closure, or acknowledgment you feel you deserve from your former spouse. I learned this the hard way during my own divorce. For years, I carried the weight of unresolved questions and lingering hopes for a final thank-you or even recognition of the positive moments we shared. It was exhausting and, honestly, it kept me stuck.

I finally realized that the closure I was seeking couldn't come from someone else—it had to come from me. This meant turning the lens inward and practicing self-examination. Before responding to my ex or acting on impulse, I started asking myself, "Will what I'm about to say or do contribute to my healing or help me move toward healthier relationships?" If the answer was no, I made the conscious choice to hold back. Trust me, it wasn't easy at first, but over time, it became a lifeline.

Lingering negative emotions are often tied to a sense of unfinished business—a longing for the other person to validate your pain or your efforts. I wanted that acknowledgment so badly, and not getting it felt like a slap in the face. But I've come to understand that healing isn't about waiting for someone else to give you what you need. The first and most important step is identifying the true source of your pain. For me, it wasn't just about the lack of acknowledgment; it was about the loss of the future I had envisioned, the dreams I had tied to our relationship.

Once I was able to name the pain, I started addressing it on my own terms. Therapy, journaling, and leaning into my support system helped me process my emotions without relying on my ex for closure. I also reframed how I viewed our shared history—not as something I needed validation for, but as a chapter in my life that shaped who I am today.

If you're navigating these same waters, remember that healing begins with you. Focus on what you can control: your actions, your thoughts, and your path forward. By letting go of the need for external acknowledgment, you free yourself to create the peace and fulfillment you truly deserve.

Can You Be Friends After Divorce?

When I reflect on my own divorce, I can say with certainty that post-divorce friendship wasn't on my mind at first. I was too caught up in the pain, confusion, and sheer exhaustion of untangling our lives. But over time, I realized that even if friendship wasn't an option, peace was.

It wasn't easy, especially with children involved. There were moments when I wanted to lash out, to blame, or to seek validation that never came. But I made a conscious decision to focus on what I could control—my actions, my words, and my commitment to creating a positive environment for my kids.

For me, taking the high road meant putting my children's needs above my own ego and finding ways to coexist peacefully with my ex. I won't sugarcoat it; there were plenty of tough days. But with time, I saw the benefits—not just for my children, but for my own sense of freedom and growth.

Whether or not friendship is possible with your ex, you can create a dynamic that's built on respect and understanding. It may not be easy, but it's worth it—for your children, for your healing, and for your future.

The end of a marriage is undeniably painful, but it doesn't have to mean the end of all communication or the possibility of maintaining some form of connection. While it's perfectly understandable that you may need time and space to heal before resuming contact with your ex, it's crucial not to cut off all ties completely. Sometimes, maintaining even limited communication can help create a sense of stability and security, not only for yourself but for your children as well. Don't dismiss the potential for a positive future, even if it looks different from what you had imagined. Every connection you hold onto can form a wider network of support, offering both you and your children a sense of love and safety that's especially needed during this turbulent time.

Consider the importance of family during this period of transition. Grandparents, aunts, uncles, and even family friends can serve as valuable sources of emotional support for your children, providing them with a safe and loving environment in the midst of the storm. Allow them the opportunity to lean on these extended family members when they need it most. The sense of continuity and stability they bring can make a world of difference, especially when your children are struggling to navigate the changes in their family dynamic.

At the same time, it's important to tread carefully when it comes to your ex's side of the family. While they may still be a part of your life, it's vital to respect their emotions and boundaries regarding the divorce. If your best friend or confidante happens to be your former in-law, it's crucial to maintain a level of sensitivity around the subject of your ex. Avoid unnecessary conversations about the divorce or any sensitive topics relating to your ex. Instead, focus on maintaining a neutral, supportive relationship, free from conflict or uncomfortable discussions. By being mindful of their feelings, you can preserve these important relationships without causing added strain.

Setting clear boundaries for yourself is a powerful tool in this process. Know what topics are off-limits and stick to them, even if it means steering conversations in a more neutral or positive direction. This will help ease any tension or discomfort that may arise, allowing you to maintain these valuable relationships without compromising your emotional well-being.

In the end, divorce doesn't have to sever all the ties that matter. With respect, clear communication, and boundaries, you can create a new version of your family dynamic—one that's built on mutual respect, emotional support, and the understanding that relationships can evolve, even after a marriage has ended. It may take time, but with patience and intention, you can navigate this challenging chapter while still providing a nurturing environment for both yourself and your children.

CHAPTER FIFTEEN

Maintaining a Positive Outlook

HEALING HEARTS - MAINTAINING A POSITIVE OUTLOOK

This chapter talks about how to maintain a positive outlook during and after a divorce, including how to cultivate gratitude, find joy in small things, and embrace a growth mindset.

Going through a divorce can be a challenging and emotionally draining experience, but it's possible to maintain a positive outlook during and after this difficult time.

Here are some strategies to help you cultivate a positive outlook:

Cultivating a Positive Outlook During and After Divorce

Divorce can feel like an emotional earthquake, shaking the foundation of your life. It disrupts your routine, alters your relationships, and forces you to reimagine your future. The pain, loss, and uncertainty may feel overwhelming, yet amidst the chaos, there lies an opportunity—a chance to rebuild, rediscover, and embrace a new version of yourself.

Maintaining a positive outlook during this transition is not just a lofty ideal; it's a lifeline to resilience, healing, and growth. This chapter delves into actionable strategies that can help you navigate divorce with grace and purpose. Through gratitude, joy in small moments, a supportive environment, a growth mindset, and self-care, you can move forward with confidence and clarity, creating a fulfilling life beyond divorce.

Practice Gratitude

When life feels like it's unraveling, gratitude may seem like a foreign concept. Divorce often magnifies feelings of loss—the loss of a partner, a shared dream, or a familiar routine. However, practicing gratitude doesn't mean ignoring your pain; it's about balancing the narrative of loss with one of abundance and hope.

Start small. Each day, identify at least one thing to be thankful for. Perhaps it's the laughter of a friend, the comfort of a warm cup of tea, or even the stability of your health. Over time, this practice rewires your brain to notice the positives, no matter how small they may seem. Research confirms that gratitude improves mental health, enhances well-being, and fosters resilience, making it an invaluable tool during tough times.

Consider keeping a gratitude journal. At the end of each day, jot down three things you're grateful for. On challenging days, revisit these entries—they serve as a testament to the enduring beauty and blessings in your life, even amid adversity.

Find Joy in Small Things

Divorce may close one chapter, but it doesn't erase life's simple pleasures. Often, it's the smallest moments that hold the most profound beauty—a golden sunset, the soothing rhythm of rain, or the laughter of a child.

Make it a practice to seek joy in the mundane. Take a moment to savor your favorite meal, immerse yourself in the melody of a song that uplifts your spirit, or relish the peaceful stillness of a quiet morning. By paying attention to these fleeting moments, you train your mind to find joy, even when life feels overwhelming.

Consider creating a "joy jar." Each time you experience a moment of happiness or peace, write it down and place it in the jar. Over time, this collection of memories becomes a treasure trove of positivity, reminding you of life's beauty, even in tough seasons.

Surround Yourself with Positivity

Your environment and the people in it have a profound impact on your outlook. During and after divorce, it's essential to cultivate a circle of positivity—individuals who uplift, support, and remind you of your worth.

Seek out friends, family members, or support groups who understand your journey and encourage your growth. Share your feelings with those who listen without judgment, offering comfort and wisdom. Their presence acts as a buffer against negativity and provides a safe space for you to heal.

Beyond relationships, curate your physical environment to reflect your healing journey. Create a home filled with things that bring you peace and joy—plants that breathe life into

Maintaining a Positive Outlook

your space, art that inspires you, or sentimental items that remind you of your strength.

Don't underestimate the power of what you consume mentally. Surround yourself with uplifting content—books that inspire, podcasts that motivate, and music that soothes your soul. Protect your mental space by setting boundaries with individuals or situations that drain your energy, focusing instead on nurturing positivity.

Embrace a Growth Mindset

Divorce is often viewed as an ending, but it's also a beginning—a chance to learn, grow, and redefine your life on your terms. A growth mindset shifts your perspective, allowing you to see challenges as opportunities for self-discovery and transformation.

Reflect on what this experience has taught you. Perhaps you've discovered inner strength you didn't know you had, or maybe it's opened your eyes to values and priorities that align more authentically with who you are. Use these lessons as stepping stones to build a future rooted in clarity and purpose.

Adopting a growth mindset also means embracing the idea that healing is a journey, not a destination. There will be setbacks, but each stumble is an opportunity to rise stronger. Set new goals—whether it's learning a skill, pursuing a passion, or building new relationships—and approach them with curiosity and determination.

Practice Self-Care

Divorce is emotionally taxing, and amidst the whirlwind, it's easy to neglect yourself. However, self-care is not a luxury; it's a necessity for your well-being and recovery.

Start with the basics. Prioritize nourishing meals, sufficient sleep, and regular exercise. These simple acts of care have a profound impact on your mental and physical health, boosting your energy and mood.

Beyond the basics, explore activities that nurture your soul. Meditation, journaling, or yoga can help you process emotions and find inner peace. Engage in hobbies that bring you joy, whether it's painting, gardening, or dancing. Self-care is deeply personal—find what works for you and make it a non-negotiable part of your routine.

Emotional self-care is equally important. Allow yourself to grieve, to feel anger, sadness, or frustration without judgment. Processing your emotions is an integral part of healing. If the weight feels too heavy, seek professional support. Therapists and counselors can provide tools and guidance to navigate this challenging period.

Finding Resilience and Renewal

The journey through and beyond divorce is not linear. There will be days of progress and days that feel like setbacks.

Remember that healing is not about erasing pain but learning to carry it with strength and grace.

By practicing gratitude, finding joy in life's small pleasures, surrounding yourself with positivity, embracing a growth mindset, and prioritizing self-care, you can cultivate a positive outlook. This outlook is not about ignoring the pain but about choosing to see the possibility beyond it—a life filled with purpose, joy, and resilience.

You are not merely surviving; you are creating a new chapter, one where you thrive. With patience, self-compassion, and determination, this chapter has the potential to be your most fulfilling yet.

Success Stories: Rebuilding Life After Divorce

Divorce can feel like the end of everything familiar—a family structure, a shared home, dreams, and even a sense of self. But it can also mark the beginning of an incredible journey of growth, self-discovery, and transformation. While the road to recovery is rarely easy, the possibilities for renewal and fulfillment are endless.

How I Reclaimed My Identity After Divorce

Divorce is more than just the end of a marriage—it's the unraveling of an identity that had been intertwined with someone else's. When I walked away from my marriage, I wasn't just leaving behind a relationship; I was stepping into an unfamiliar world where I had to redefine who I was outside of being a spouse. It was both terrifying and liberating.

The Journey Back to Myself

Reclaiming my identity wasn't an instant process—it was a journey of self-discovery, one step at a time. At first, I felt lost, unsure of where to even begin. But slowly, I started peeling back the layers, rediscovering the woman I had been before marriage—and the person I was meant to become.

Reconnecting with My Passions

One of the first things I did was revisit the hobbies and interests I had set aside. I started journaling again, pouring out my thoughts onto the pages, using writing as a way to heal. I spent time in nature, going for walks and even starting a garden with my children. We created the most beautiful rose garden in the neighborhood, a small but powerful reminder that beauty can grow from struggle.

Rediscovering My Independence

For years, I had made decisions as part of a couple. Now, I had to relearn how to trust myself. The first time I made a major decision on my own, I felt uncertain. But with each choice—big or small—I gained confidence. I realized that I was capable, strong, and resourceful.

Setting New Goals

With my marriage behind me, I had the opportunity to dream again. What did I want for myself? Where did I see my future going? I sat down and made a list of personal and professional goals—some small, some ambitious. Slowly, I started working toward them, proving to myself that life wasn't just about survival—it was about growth.

Surrounding Myself with the Right People

Not everyone understood my journey. Some friends drifted away, unable to relate to my new reality. But I also found new connections—people who encouraged me, who reminded me of my worth, who didn't define me by my past. I learned that the relationships I chose to keep had to be ones that lifted me up, not ones that kept me stuck.

Redefining My Self-Worth

One of the biggest shifts I made was learning to value myself outside of my roles as a wife or mother. My worth wasn't tied to my marital status, my financial situation, or my past mistakes. It was rooted in who I was as a person—the love I gave, the strength I carried, and the resilience I built through every hardship.

How *You* Can Reclaim *Your* Identity

If you are going through a similar journey, know that you are not alone. Here are some steps you can take to reclaim your identity after divorce:

- ✅ Explore What Makes You Happy – Take time to revisit old hobbies or try new ones. Whether it's painting, reading, traveling, or learning something new, give yourself the space to rediscover what brings you joy.

- ✅ Make Decisions for Yourself – Start small, like choosing how to spend your weekend, and work up to bigger decisions. The more you trust yourself, the stronger your confidence will become.

- ✅ Set Goals for Your Future – Write down things you want to accomplish, no matter how big or small. Having a vision for your future can help guide you toward a fulfilling new chapter.

- ✅ Surround Yourself with Supportive People – Find a support system of friends, family, or even a therapist who uplift you and encourage your growth.

- ✅ Define Your Own Worth – Remember, your value isn't defined by your past relationship. Focus on the qualities that make you unique and embrace the person you are becoming.

Embracing Your New Identity

Reclaiming my identity after divorce wasn't just about rediscovering who I used to be—it was about stepping into a new, stronger version of myself. The woman who emerged from this process wasn't just surviving; she was thriving. She had learned to stand on her own, to trust herself, and to embrace the future with open arms.

Divorce may have closed one chapter, but it didn't define my entire story. In fact, it gave me the chance to write a new one—one where I was the main character, fully in control of my own narrative. And that, I realized, was the greatest gift of all.

If you're on this journey too, take your time. Explore what makes you happy. Surround yourself with people who uplift you. And most importantly, believe in yourself. Your identity isn't gone—it's just waiting to be rediscovered.

Journaling: A Tool for Growth

Keeping a journal became an essential part of my healing journey. Writing provided a safe space to express my emotions without fear of judgment.

Research shows that journaling improves mood, helps process trauma, and fosters a sense of control. For me, it became a way to track my growth and focus on the positive. My entries often included simple joys:

- The warmth of the sun on my face.

- A heartfelt compliment from a friend.

- A meal that reminded me of home.

These small moments added up, helping me shift my perspective and focus on gratitude. Journaling became not just a tool for healing but a practice I continue to this day.

Steps Toward a Happy Life

Divorce often challenges mental health, but it also offers an opportunity for renewal. Here are some strategies that helped me build a fulfilling life post-divorce:

- **Engage in Activities You Love:** Rediscover old hobbies or try something new. I rekindled my love for painting, which became a therapeutic outlet.

- **Prioritize Self-Care:** Nurture your physical and emotional well-being. A simple walk in nature can work wonders.

- **Seek Support:** Whether from friends, family, or professionals, surround yourself with people who uplift you.

- **Set Goals:** Focus on personal growth, and celebrate every milestone, no matter how small.

- **Practice Gratitude:** Cultivate a mindset that appreciates life's blessings, even during tough times.

Wrapping Up

Divorce can feel like an insurmountable challenge, but it doesn't mean the end of happiness. By embracing self-discovery, focusing on growth, and finding joy in small moments, you can rebuild your life in a way that reflects your resilience and strength.

The journey takes time, patience, and self-compassion, but the result is worth it—a life that is rich with possibility, purpose, and joy. Remember, your story is still unfolding. The best chapters are yet to come.

The Ultimate Guide to Finding Freedom After Divorce: Free Checklist

Congratulations on taking the first step towards finding freedom and embracing a new chapter in your life. Use this checklist to navigate the journey ahead and make the most out of your post-divorce transformation.

Self-Reflection and Rediscovery:

- ☐ Reflect on your past and identify key lessons learnt from your past.

- ☐ List your strengths, passions, and values.

- ☐ Set personal goals for the next chapter of your life.

Emotional Healing:
- ☐ Acknowledge and accept your emotions.
- ☐ Seek support from friends, family, or a therapist.
- ☐ Practice self-care regularly.

Co-Parenting and Child Custody:
- ☐ Establish open communication with your ex-spouse.
- ☐ Create a flexible co-parenting plan.
- ☐ Prioritize your children's well-being.

Positive Co-Parenting Relationship:
- ☐ Foster a respectful and cooperative attitude.
- ☐ Set boundaries and maintain consistency.
- ☐ Focus on effective communication for the children's sake.

Dating After Divorce:
- ☐ Take time for self-discovery before entering a new relationship.
- ☐ Establish clear boundaries and communicate expectations.
- ☐ Consider seeking advice from those who have navigated post-divorce dating successfully.

Financial Independence:
- ☐ Evaluate your financial situation.

- ☐ Create a budget and financial goals.

- ☐ Explore opportunities for career advancement or additional income streams.

Building a Support System:
- ☐ Cultivate a network of friends who understand and support you.

- ☐ Join support groups or online communities for divorced individuals.

- ☐ Be open to seeking professional help if needed.

Healing and Moving On:
- ☐ Embrace forgiveness and let go of resentment.

- ☐ Focus on personal growth and self-improvement.

- ☐ Engage in activities that bring you joy and fulfillment.

Redefining Your Relationships:
- ☐ Reevaluate and set boundaries in toxic relationships.

- ☐ Cultivate healthy relationships that align with your values.

- ☐ Communicate openly and honestly in your relationships.

Maintaining a Positive Outlook:

☐ Practice gratitude daily.

☐ Stay optimistic about your future.

☐ Surround yourself with positivity and inspirational content.

Success Stories:

☐ Seek inspiration from the success stories of others who have found freedom after divorce.

☐ Connect with individuals who have navigated similar challenges successfully.

☐ Celebrate your own victories along the way.

Embrace the Present with Gratitude

Be mindful of the present and appreciate all that you have. Everything happens for a reason—even if you don't understand it at the moment, trust that the universe is guiding you. Challenges may seem difficult, but they often serve to clear the path for better days ahead.

Believe in the power of positivity, as the universe is always listening and aligning things in your favor.

Vashtie Doorga
Doorga Entertainment
647-921-216

Navigating Divorce with Financial Confidence

Divorce is a challenging and emotionally taxing experience, especially for women. Seeking guidance from a trusted financial specialist or advisor can provide clarity on your current financial situation and help you plan for a secure future.

Key steps to consider:

- Review your financial standing and create a roadmap for your next chapter.
- Update your **will** and **power of attorney** to reflect your current wishes.
- Ensure beneficiary information is updated on **life insurance policies** and **registered investments**.

Above all, stay positive, practice self-care, and be kind to yourself during this transition.

Anjali Jaggan RRC
Fund Investment Specialist
Co-Operators Financial Investment Services Inc.
905-415-8000 | Anjali_jaggan@cooperators.ca

Sandy Maeck
EMPOWER YOU
BE EMPOWERED TO REACH YOUR GOALS
AND LIVE YOUR BEST LIFE
Life Coach
Renowned Author
Motivational Speaker
Expert Workshop Facilitator
Offers
the unwanted wife
SANDY MAECK
unhitched
the ungracious daughter
the condemned one
Failure to Launch
SANDY MAECK
4167223998
sandy@sandymaeck.com
www.sandymaeck.com

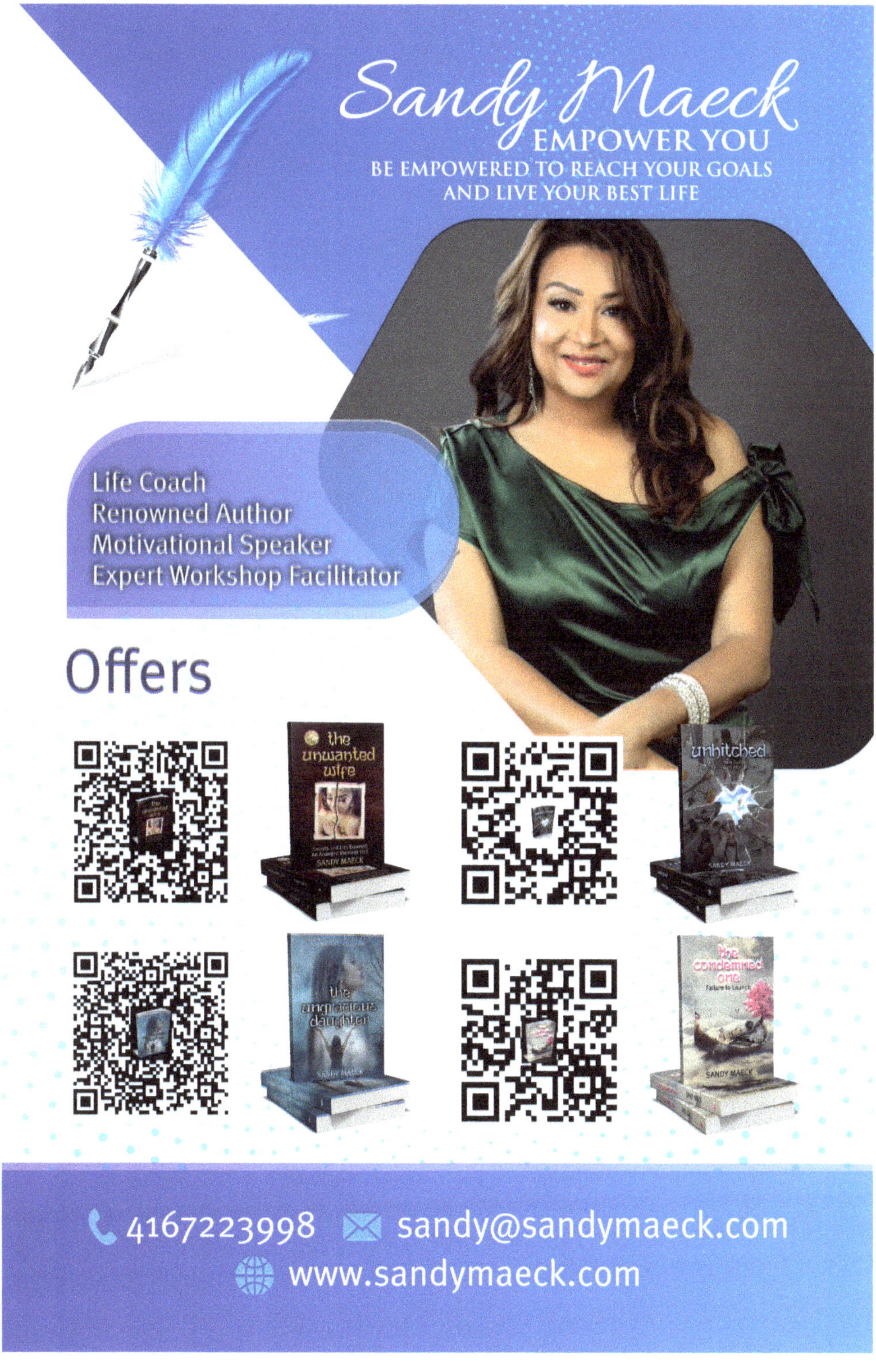

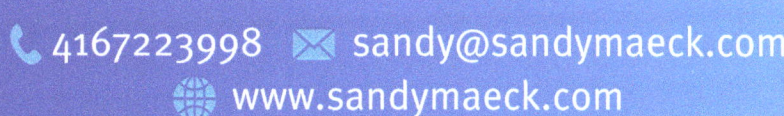

Sandy Maeck

AUTHOR | LIFE COACH | SPEAKER | ADVOCATE
SURVIVOR. WARRIOR. VOICE FOR CHANGE

Sandy Maeck is a powerhouse of resilience, transformation, and empowerment. A bestselling author, life coach, and the visionary CEO and founder of **Empower You** and **STCC Dance Academy**, she has dedicated her life to inspiring others to rise above adversity.

A Story of Survival & Strength

More than a survivor—Sandy is a warrior. A mother, wife, grandmother, and business leader, she has turned her personal battles into a mission to uplift and empower. Her bestselling books — **The Unwanted Wife** and **The Ungracious Daughter** — are raw, unflinching accounts of **domestic violence, arranged marriage, narcissistic abuse, and betrayal.**

Her latest works, **Unhitched: The Ultimate Guide to Surviving Divorce** and **The Condemned One**, delve into the emotional scars of trauma, mental health struggles, and epilepsy, proving that even in the darkest moments, resilience prevails.

Sandy's personal journey mirrors the stories she tells. **She has endured. She has fought. And she has won.** Now, she stands as a guiding light for those still trapped in the shadows.

Empowering Others Through Action

As the founder of **Empower You by Sandy Maeck**, Sandy is on a mission to help women break free, reclaim their power, and create the change they deserve. Through coaching, advocacy, and mentorship, she equips women with the tools to transform their lives—because survival is just the beginning.

At the same time, through **STCC Dance Academy**, Sandy merges her passion for the arts with her drive for advocacy. She volunteers her time mentoring youth and adults, using movement as a tool for healing, empowerment, and self-expression. Her tireless dedication has earned her multiple civic and volunteer awards, proving that her impact extends far beyond the pages of her books.

Inspirational Speaker & Thought Leader

With a commanding presence and an unfiltered, powerful message, Sandy ignites transformation wherever she speaks. Her talks are raw, moving, and deeply empowering.

- ✓ Surviving Domestic Violence & Abuse
- ✓ Reclaiming Power After Trauma
- ✓ Healing Through Writing
- ✓ Breaking Free from Narcissistic Abuse
- ✓ Custom Talks Tailored to Any Audience

As a fierce advocate, Sandy also provides **one-on-one consultations** for women navigating the aftermath of abuse, equipping them with the tools to rebuild and thrive.

Book Sandy for Your Next Event
Your past doesn't define you—your courage does.

📞 (416) 722-3998   ✉ sandy@sandymaeck.com   🌐 www.sandymaeck.com

Your past doesn't define you—your courage does.

Notes

Unhitched

Notes

www.ingramcontent.com/pod-product-compliance
Lightning Source LLC
Chambersburg PA
CBHW061215070526
44584CB00029B/3844